Stories Savory and Sweet

Stories Savory and Sweet

Margie Zats

NODIN PRESS

Acknowledgments
With appreciation to Kay Carda for her excellent technical
assistance. And to my sometimes laughable, always loveable
relatives who, by just being themselves, gave me so much
material to write about. Thanks you all!

ISBN: 978-1-947237-45-2
Library of Congress Control Number: 2022942384

Published by
Nodin Press
210 Edge Place, Minneapolis,
55418

www.nodinpress.com

Printed in USA

Dedicated to my son Jonathan
who guided my hand

Contents

PREFACE

Golden leaves fluttered downward, abandoning the privilege of summer, acknowledging the season of life.

Standing at my window, my mind meandered across a cloudless sky into the land of memories, recalling people who would never be famous and small events too insignificant for some but important to me.

I knew then that I must safeguard these reflections, those observations and experiences I have lived long enough to acquire. I owed it to my grandchildren and to the people I have yet to meet. I could offer them the gift of laughter and perhaps, the softness of an unexpected tear.

As each leaf flies fancifully on the whim of a breeze, the various characters in these stories emerge throughout. Unique and individual, they do not intermingle with one another, but gathered together like a handful of fallen foliage they produce a bountiful array.

Enjoy!

A BASKET CASE

O nly the whimsy of genetics has prevented me from becoming the next Michael Jordan. In my mind I had potential but, unfortunately, being a foot too short and a light-year too slow kept me from an impressive career on the bas-ketball court.

When you read this you'll agree.

Though I could barely pass Phys. Ed in school, I was nonetheless a friendly girl, and throughout the years I main-tained camaraderie with a young woman who had the good fortune of marrying the owner of an NBA team.

She often invited me to join them. I sat through games as if my head was on a swivel, watching the two competitors plunge the ball into the basket. I shouted words of encourage-ment but refrained from verbalizing criticism. I figured the guys felt badly enough without confirmation from me.

The seasons continued, winning and losing.

One early spring day my friend called.

"Would you like to fly with the team to a game on the East Coast?"

I accepted before she finished the sentence.

A few weeks later we drove to the charter air terminal to board the private jet. Men as tall as trees were already assem-bled and boarding the front of the plane. We visitors respect-fully waited our turns to fill the back of the aircraft.

Amazingly, with all that weight, we lifted off, and the passengers were told dinner was being served.

I approached the buffet with my usual healthy appetite, anticipating delicious cuisine. There were trays of appetizers, but as I reached down, my hand was eclipsed by an enormous paw. Never had I seen such a scope. This man-giant, who could encompass a basketball in one palm, had taken possession of an entire tray, leaving only the fringe of a lettuce leaf for others.

"Excuse me," I said meekly. But manners were obscured by the need to feed a ravenous cavern. He ignored me and continued to abscond with the platter's contents, denuding all but the relishes.

What could I do against this rival who could squash a squash with one hand? So I quietly filled my plate with olives and pickles and the two slices of pepperoni he'd overlooked. I went back to my seat, glad to remember that I had peppermints in my purse.

After landing we were driven to the hotel, the players in the first bus and we tagalongs in the second.

By the next morning I was determined to have a farmer's breakfast. Mints are not a satisfying entrée.

As I stepped into the elevator, three members of the team were there. I said a cheery "good morning" and then, out of nowhere, an amusing anecdote came to me. Intending to regale them, I began, knowing I had a captive audience for the ride down.

The year before, I had been sitting in bed watching TV and eating a banana. As I took the last bite, I carefully folded the peel into a compact bundle. I don't know what possessed me but after surveying the wastebasket across the room, I released the peel and with the flip of the wrist, hurled it through the air and smacked it right into the receptacle. Pow! It landed with a resonating thud.

I retold my moment of triumph with all the confidence of a champion. Only my audience didn't seem to be impressed. Actually, no one reacted at all. One fellow stared at the elevator signal as though he willed it to hurry. The others stood in silence, waiting for the door to open to escape.

Undaunted, I bid them farewell with the promise I'd attend their game that evening.

And so I did, content in the thought I'd given them a challenge. Yes, those pros can whirl and twirl magic with a basketball. They can win trophies and endorse sneakers and sign autographs for adoring fans. But in the hour of judgment, how many of them could outsmart a piece of fruit?

A Fake and a Cake

The wall was white. And no description of vanilla or snowflake or buttercream could enhance its plainness. It was, to all observation, basic white. Adding to its bleakness was the reality that it served no purpose, just mundane footage that led to another room while holding up the ceiling.

A constant challenge, the space the wall enclosed was too small for any furniture placement. I considered hanging a painting there although the adjacent rooms held too many already. I needed something new, an innovation, a conversation piece.

Whether in frustration or absentmindedness, I glanced out to my yard and saw a tree in all of nature's splendor, its branches stretching upwards; and I felt inspired that I, too, could extend myself.

Could an object of such beauty be brought inside? And more to the point, who sells a good fake? A Big Box store was the answer, one-stop shopping that carries merchandise ranging from cases of cream of mushroom soup to replicas of everything else.

Admittedly, I could have shopped at an established nursery, but that would have required coping with tangled roots and dead leaves as well as my tendency to over-water. Coddling an actual tree was beyond my limitations.

The store was a quick drive. The parking lot was full, making it necessary to leave my car on the fringe. I grabbed a cart and walked directly to the far end where I'd seen faux plants displayed. Among the bouquets and wreaths were fir trees and chintzy pots holding compliant foliage with synthetic leaves and branches large enough to hide behind if necessary.

Initially discouraged, I kept searching until I saw, against the metal racks, my honey. The tree was leaning snuggly against the third shelf, making me wonder which one was holding the other up. With a yank at the base, I plunged this jolly green giant into my cart and proceeded to the cashier to make the purchase. After tucking my credit card safely away, I headed out the door towards my car. That's when reality hit me. How could I shove a jungle into the back seat of a compact? I stood there, in the midst of swerving traffic, and looked up to the sky, expecting the cloud formation to somehow spell out the answer.

"Do you need some help?" called a voice across the crowd.

I could see a middle-aged woman approaching as I gestured an open-armed welcome. She stared at the tree; she stared at my car. She saw the expression on my face and needed no explanation. I offered one anyway to which she responded.

"I have that SUV over there. Where do you live? I'll take it home for you."

I relayed my address, interspersed with nods of approval, and within minutes this Good Samaritan had snatched up the tree and aimed it towards her large trunk.

I then got into my automobile and drove slowly home, hoping I would continue to see her following in the rearview mirror. I didn't. I began to worry about what I'd just agreed to. The tree was not cheap. It had already been charged to my

Visa. What if this apparent do-gooder also had a white wall in her house and was plotting to abscond with my décor? I drove into my driveway, reluctant to glance behind me, anticipating only tire marks on asphalt. The roar of an engine was a welcome relief as I saw the SUV pull in.

Together we carried the tree up the steps and through the hallway, gently putting it in place. The white wall became illuminated as green, nature's chlorophyll, brightened the area and glamorized the orphaned space.

This stranger standing beside me, a woman I had known for twenty minutes, suddenly became my best friend. She smiled as I thanked her profusely.

"May I pay you for helping me?"

"Oh no," she was quick to reply.

"But what can I do to return the favor? What's your favorite charity? I insist on reciprocating."

She thought for a moment before responding.

"Well, my mother recently had a fatal heart attack and…"

"I'll send a donation in her memory to the Heart Association."

Suddenly I realized I hadn't even asked her name.

"Please write down what I need to know."

She searched her purse, retrieving a scrap of paper on which she jotted the necessary information.

I took it from her without glancing down and shoved the paper into the pocket of my jacket.

Again we smiled as we walked together towards the door.

As I expressed my appreciation for perhaps the hundredth time, the woman left, apparently anxious to be on her way (or escape my repetitive chatter).

Days passed, and the tree that would never bloom in the spring fulfilled its obligation. The white wall was aptly disguised. As promised, I sent a check to the American Heart Association and, after receiving the customary "thank you," assumed my promise was fulfilled and that the whole experience would fade into history.

So I thought. One morning soon after, the phone rang. I didn't recognize the caller at first, but it was my tree friend.

"Oh Margie, I cannot believe this coincidence. Let me tell you!"

"So tell me."

She continued, "The Heart Association sent a letter regarding your contribution in Mom's name. I had to read it twice before it all sunk in. Then I realized I had never asked your name. I couldn't believe this could happen."

"What could happen? Please explain."

"'My mother frequently attended your culinary classes. She enjoyed baking and loved your recipes. In fact, your special apple cake was her favorite. She made it so often for family dinners. My sister and I decided to serve it at the luncheon after her memorial. We knew she would have liked that, and the family was so comforted by the sweet memories."

Suddenly I felt wrapped in warmth on a frosty Minnesota morning. This stranger, someone I chanced upon in a Big Box parking lot, had offered me assistance, a pair of helping hands while I, unknowingly, had given her mother a pleasure. I felt humbled to have had the opportunity.

After marveling at the happy ending, I recited a short horticultural review of "our" tree's condition. It was holding up well. We then closed the conversation without making plans to meet again, knowing we were only ships passing in the night.

And so, this woman and the now renowned cake were relegated to an anecdote to re-tell whenever there was a lull in conversation at a party. Perhaps, somewhere in the city, my Good Samaritan has also retold the story to her friends, adding her own flourishes.

Some years later, it was time to sell the house and downsize. I sold the tree cheaply at a garage sale (advising the new owner to occasionally wipe the leaves with a damp cloth). My new place can only accommodate basic seating and eating. There are no awkward spaces to fill or lonesome white walls.

Thinking back, could we dismiss all of this as coincidental, merely a happenstance meeting of two people being in the same place at the same time? Has nostalgia softened our logic, or was there a sprinkling of magic tossed from above? Perhaps it's best not to delve deeper.

Today the delectable aroma of warm apple cake, bursting with butter and cinnamon, still delights me and nourishes the memories of an ordinary day that became special.

Whether with words that make headlines or a quiet act that needs no words, we are touched with the pleasure of a gift always cherished yet seldom encountered—a Random Act of Kindness.

Fresh Apple Torte

⅓ cup flour
⅓ cup sugar
½ teaspoon baking soda
½ teaspoon cinnamon
1 extra large egg
1 cup lite sour cream
½ cup apricot jam
2 tablespoons lemon juice
3 tablespoons butter, melted
3 large apples, peeled, cored, sliced thin
¾ cup golden raisins
Vanillan soken (vanilla sugar)*

Beat together first 9 ingredients until well-blended. Stir in apples and raisins. Pour mixture evenly into Walnut Crust. Bake at 350°, 40 minutes. Cool before serving.

Decorate with vanilla sugar.

Walnut Crust

1 cup flour
1 cup dark brown sugar, firmly packed
½ cup butter, softened
½ cup walnuts, chopped

Beat together flour, sugar and butter until mixture resembles coarse meal. Stir in walnuts. Pat evenly on bottom of 10" spring form pan. Bake at 350°, 8 minutes. Cool 5 minutes before filling. Serves 8.

*Vanillan soken can be found in the baking department of the grocery store.

Amore Mio

Did I ever tell you about the affair I didn't have with a famous movie star?

It began simply enough at that lunch in Rome. I'd taken my sons to Italy hoping to inspire them with history and art. They were young, eager to absorb the culture of the Eternal City—and hungry most of the time.

That's where he saw me, seated at a table in the hotel dining room. The kids and I had checked into the Hilton the night before. I was exhausted from the long flight and not yet accustomed to the humidity that untamed my curly hair and flushed my face.

I ordered us tall glasses of something soothing as we waited for our food. We were seated at an indoor table directly across from the French doors that opened onto the patio. I sat facing the lovely garden view and noticed the table in the center of the doorway. It was directly in our line of vision. I instantly recognized the man at the table—Burt Lancaster, the Hollywood Hunk. Just then one of us spilled and another started complaining, and my attention was diverted to child care.

We ate, we laughed, and like all tourists, we talked about which of the famous ruins to visit that afternoon. Unexpectedly my son seated next to me whispered words I will never forget.

"Burt Lancaster has been staring at you, Mom."

I couldn't believe the kid, but I'd never known him to lie, so apparently it was true.

I replied quietly that I was aware he also was a guest at the hotel because we'd seen him earlier walking through the lobby.

I'd noticed how slender he looked, but then I remembered the camera adds ten pounds. He had always appeared so muscular in his movies. No longer the vigorous circus performer of his youth, he was now an actor of handsome maturity.

I sat there, sprinkling Parmesan cheese on my fettuccini, as I basked in the gaze of a man who'd seen the legends of Hollywood.

I needed to make a decision: should I keep eating, or acknowledge his attention? Of course I couldn't resist. I looked up, stared straight at him and for seconds our eyes met—until he looked away. Our tryst was over. I'd blown it. But that look in his eyes will remain seared within me, deep and intense, belonging only to me for a moment in time.

Fantasies danced in my head. Here I was, a stranger across a crowded room, and there he sat, admiring my obvious charms. I imagined he'd scribble a note on a paper napkin, sending it with the waiter. Only three words. I'd read quickly, and my smile would answer "yes." The three words: "Ditch the kids."

Could I, would I, dare to abandon my maternal obligations and pay a tour guide double lire to keep the children on a city-wide sightseeing bus?

Stolen hours with Burt. We'd spend the afternoon

together languishing under the sultry Roman sun, sipping Chianti and sharing the thrill of it all.

My youngest son tugged at my sleeve, forcing me back to reality, to accept what never would be.

We finished lunch, and as I walked towards the door, I allowed myself a glance back to the patio. His table was empty, except for a waiter clearing the empty dishes. All trace of his ever having been there had vanished like a flicker on the silver screen.

Within weeks our European adventure ended, and we returned to life as we knew it. I told my friends about my tête-à-tête with Burt Lancaster (adding a touch of drama each time). But it didn't go well. Cynics offered sensible explanations.

"Perhaps he looked at you and thought 'that poor woman with those crazy kids. No wonder she looks so tired!'"

Someone else suggested he was just gazing into space.

I attributed their comments to jealousy. They joked while I kept his image safely stored in the attic of my mind. Although he was a bit skinny, I remained impressed.

I assumed Burt had gone back to Beverly Hills, surrounding himself with a bevy of beauties. Half a globe away from that table in Rome, he gave no thought to the woman whose eyes met his. She had long been demoted to a momentary encounter. He was unaware that he would never again see the flash of her marinara-stained smile.

Fate can be unkind. With all his fame and fortune, Burt was never to know that this woman (with the rowdy kids) could have been his happy ending.

As they write on the final page of the script, as the camera captures the silhouette of a man standing alone against a fading sunset, we hear him sigh, "Where is my woman? Our flame is unrequited."

Others may wonder—but I will know—those words are meant for me. For I am that woman he's longed for, destined to remain forever "the one that got away."

Adieu, amore mio, adieu.

Cue the violins.

A Table Fable

It was hiding in full sight, as though this inanimate object sensed the moment of its Grande Revelation, waiting, oh so patiently, for the right day, the correct time to allow its elegance to be discovered.

"Oh Ronnie, I do love this dining room table! Look at the quality of the wood, the rich patina and the sculptural legs; it must have been handmade by an artisan. I've never seen a set so stunning. I ... we must buy it, whatever the cost!"

A soprano voice soared through the showroom permeating the hallway, extending into the outer reception area of the Fine Classics Furniture store.

Other shoppers stopped their conversations momentarily, not only because their voices could not compete, but to smile at one another as they imagined unseen "Ronnie" confronting an astronomical price tag.

Muffled syllables from a determined salesman could not be deciphered by nearby customers, but the emphatic tone imposed was evidence he had no intention of allowing this commission to escape. Anxious to close the deal, he looked straight at the couple and spoke with an almost spiritual reverence.

"Dine in splendor. A truly memorable experience for you and your guests to enjoy together."

Ronnie (who routinely succumbed to his wife's requests) didn't have a chance. So with a shrug of resignation, he opened his wallet, removed a well-worn credit card and relinquished it to the eager salesman.

His wife smiled approvingly as she gently glided her fingertips across the table's glossy cherrywood veneer before proceeding to brush her husband's cheek with a kiss.

The remaining customers left the store that day never to know "the Ronnies"—or if they would dine, always and forever, in splendor.

Two robust-looking men in matching beige jumpsuits moved effortlessly to hoist the piece furniture into a van.

"The tag on that table says there's a couple of leaves, too!" hollered the younger one as he climbed onto the driver's seat. His partner turned to grab the missing boards. Fine Classics Furniture was written on the back of his uniform. A walking advertisement wherever he went all day. Driving out to the suburbs would take over half an hour, more if traffic was heavy or the late afternoon trucks clogged the freeway. "Who wants to live out this far" was uttered more as a statement than a question. One agreed with the other.

It was nearing five when the van turned into the cul-de-sac. Mammoth homes, obviously large enough for families with ten children, sprawled for blocks. Only there were no designated blocks. There weren't even any sidewalks, only a wide-paved road leading up to three-car garages.

"There it is, that one with the big bay window and all those flowers up front." As the van pulled up, the front door opened and, presumably, the lady of the house emerged, waving her hand to indicate she was anxious to speak.

"You're finally here! I've been waiting for hours! You have my beautiful table. Please be careful with it."

The woman motioned them to the front French doors, apparently the widest entrance to the house. Fluttering ahead, she escorted the deliverymen into the dining room, instructed them to place the table directly under the gleaming crystal chandelier, and asked if they wanted a drink of water. Wiping their perspiring brows with their sleeves, they declined, explaining they were used to heavy lifting and really needed to leave. The three then walked back into the foyer, and as the men departed, our homeowner (whose name we'll get to later) was compelled to glance at her image in the entranceway mirror. Displeased with hair that had tousled in the breeze outdoors, she shrugged disapprovingly, then backtracked to the dining room to admire its recent acquisition.

The setting sun beamed its rays upon the table's bronze-colored surface. She sighed, then smiled. Tonight lists would be compiled; guests would be evaluated. A selection of relatives, friends, and business associates would become candidates for invitations to her memorable dinner parties. She would bask in admiration as the most gracious hostess. The daydreams banged to a close as the mechanical gears of a garage door rolled open and Ronnie announced he was, "Home, dear."

"Rachel, where are you?" Ronnie hollered twice before his wife (who preferred the more exotic "Racquel" ever since she took a class in Latin dancing) responded. He was to meet her in the dining room so together they could view their latest purchase—she with the expectation of grandeur, he with the anticipation of a bill on the first of the month.

"Oh Ron, isn't it elegant?" Not waiting for a reply, Racquel continued. "Imagine our porcelain tureen filled with vichyssoise, gorgeous under the glow of the chandelier."

Ronnie, worn from a lengthy day of business, could only nod at the thought of shimmering potato soup. His wife continued extolling fanciful images as her husband gently guided her to the kitchen where tonight's spaghetti waited in a pot on the stove.

And so it was—Racquel spent long hours composing lists of suitable companions: new friends they'd met at the club, long-time acquaintances with successful careers, and anyone on the top rung of the social ladder who could be a potential asset.

A routine developed. The Chosen would gather at seven, and after a few martinis, be ushered into the dimly-lit dining room. Ron never did understand why the chandelier was set on low after all the fuss about "glowing brightly." He did not, however, ask.

The place cards were sorted to separate husbands and wives rather than seat them together. Racquel enjoyed explaining that this was deliberate so that conversations would remain fresh and lively. In truth, she placed the more attractive men next to herself.

Course by course was served. The white wine with the smoked salmon was replaced by a robust red to compliment the Boeuf Wellington. Hired servers moved deftly between chairs without spilling a drop of sauce or permitting a sprig of parsley to reposition itself.

As nine o'clock became ten, guests were instructed to exchange places, much like a game played in childhood. Each person assumed a different chair to initiate a scintillating conversation to the left or right of their choosing. This procedure would continue until it was time to go home.

"Thank-you's" filled the foyer. As the front door finally closed, Racquel reiterated the adjectives to Ron's back as he hurriedly departed for the kitchen, aware that the evening's hired help was waiting to be paid. His wife, continuing to float on her compliments, then turned out the lights, pausing briefly at the now serene dining room. With a sigh of contentment, the glittering lighting was shut off as its owners climbed up the stairs, quite worn from the evening's drama.

One event became a series. It could be said that eventually the dinners became a lifestyle. No one refused Racquel's invitations. It was rumored many guests arranged their traveling or canceled other plans to be available. Other than a wedding or funeral, all who were invited attended.

Racquel was in her glory. Ron was in debt. The dinners were costing a fortune. However, the contacts and faux friendships were of some value. Racquel was asked to serve on committees of charity galas, and Ron opened new accounts. But with regret, the "merry-go-round's" momentum gradually slowed to a repetitive pace.

"Enough already! I'm tired of meeting the florist in the driveway and paying the grocery bill for a small nation! For God's sake, Rachel, can't we just have a bowl of soup and watch a movie?"

His wife, to his surprise, stood silent, unable to answer. Unable to deny what she, too, had been reluctant to admit. No, not about the florist, but the constant pressure to produce such evenings. It had become too much. This filet mignon in puff pastry was taking a bite out of her. She was working too hard to make an impression on those who ultimately didn't matter. Words she had never before used, feelings she had never confessed, tumbled out.

"And it all started with that damn fancy table! A hunk of wood a carpenter put together." Rachel, Racquel was basically a good person. Maybe too anxious to attain status but otherwise well meaning, and in her heart still in love with her husband. She felt tears forming. A single drop trickled down her cheek with a waterfall to come.

"Oh Ronnie, what have I done to us? Where did I ..."

"We," he interrupted. Further words were not needed because each felt the anguish of the other.

"The last supper is done, over." She spoke as if it were a declaration.

"I'll tell that to Da Vinci." And they both broke into laughter.

The years passed, and the beautiful table stood idle, used only for small family gatherings and, of course, Thanksgiving. Ronnie looked forward to retirement and Rachel (once again) was content to volunteer at their children's school. In time she was out of a job as those children became adults and went on their way.

The house seemed to have grown larger, with too many empty rooms echoing silence. The intrusive chill of winter could not compete with the warmth of Arizona, so they decided to call a realtor and move west.

Most of the furniture was sold at an estate sale, but the glittering chandelier remained for the next occupants to keep dusted. Its companion, the prized table, presented a problem—too large for the new condo in Scottsdale but a family heirloom too sentimental to relinquish.

By some great celestial plan, their oldest daughter and young family had recently purchased a house in the city. The contemporary architecture featured a large Great Room, a combination kitchen and lounge area. Certainly no space for an imposing table.

Rachel, reverting back to her Racquel days, was not to be deterred.

"Betsy, darling, I want you to take it."

"Take what?"

"The table, sweetheart. The gorgeous table."

"That clunker? Where am I supposed to put it?"

"You'll find space. I'll come over and help you rearrange."

Her daughter grimaced. "If you absolutely insist, I'll take it."

"You'll love it, Betsy. I promise."

Betsy and her husband spent the next weekend trans-figuring the Great Room. If they eliminated his large lounge chair and the bookcase too, there would be enough space.

"Where am I going to watch the games now?"

"Don't worry, Ken, we'll do a man cave in the basement for you. Otherwise, go argue with my mother."

"No chance. I'd rather take the basement."

Rachel got her way, Betsy made arrangements, and the table found a new home. The chairs presented a separate chal-lenge. The woven cane seats would never survive the results of a baseball field and the grunge of jeans making it to third base."

Betsy immediately purchased large plastic chair pads for protection. Ties on each chair leg dangled freely under the somewhat matching cloth that covered the entire table, insur-ing its longevity. By some stretch of décor, the design repeated the pads' palette, although no one could ever discern if the border of red circles was apples or tomatoes.

Gone were the silver trays laden with expensive out-of-season fruits. Gone was the gold-edged English china, service for twelve. All had been replaced with sturdy pottery and an assortment of vagabond mugs.

Betsy tried hard to safeguard her inheritance, remembering back to those elegant dinner parties upon which her mother's life revolved. How she'd giggle, half hidden on the stairway, peeking out from behind the banister, to gaze at the fancy dressed-up ladies. Fascinated. But as little girls do, her yawning would soon give her secret away, and being discovered, she'd be shooed up to bed.

There were occasions, such as family celebrations, when she had a rightful place at the table, dinners when she was the designated recipient of the good stuff. But that wasn't as much fun as sitting at the kitchen counter where she could spill. Her children would never know the experience of fine dining, or the pressure that went with choosing the right fork.

The table began as an unwelcome intruder, but eventually the family wondered how they ever got along without it.

Each child was assigned their place. The two older boys required separation because of their tendency to kick each other when the opportunity arose.

When the tabletop wasn't covered with food, it became a landscape of technology. And when it wasn't the recipient of communications, it made a splendid catch-all for keys, unread mail and other goods of unknown origin.

Many a birthday cake and small triumph was joyfully celebrated as the years progressed.

"What did you learn in school today?" was replaced by talk of colleges, and then careers, marriages, and singleness. The family unit diminished, leaving one less chair at the table until only a single place remained.

No longer used for meals, the once-polished veneer bore an obvious scar from Betsy's coffee mug placed there often and carelessly.

Too preoccupied to notice, she had opened an online business, and until it was successful enough to rent office space, the old table would have to suffice. Scattered papers, charts, lists, and ledgers were spread to each edge—along with that half-filled cup of coffee gone cold.

Her family had dispersed, and as history has a way of repeating itself, the house was put on the market. Though much of the furniture was disposed of, the table still whispered of its former elegance. And with thoughts of her mother, Betsy couldn't let it be sold at the garage sale.

A nearby school, the same one her children had attended, came to mind. Betsy called the principal with an offer he couldn't refuse. Within days, three brawny young fellows (undoubtedly part of the football team) came to haul the table away. It would reside in the teachers' lounge to be used daily for lunch as well as for frequent staff meetings. Betsy was delighted, the school personnel were pleased, and a new purpose was given to the wood.

The students would never know how their futures were discussed or overhear the frustrations about despondent kids, or how to best help the ones with learning disabilities. Ideas flying across a table (once used for potluck suppers) became a debate arena. Which techniques could reach the unreachable, the ones who thought they knew it all.

Amazingly, the steadfast table did not wobble, though the sunlight flowing into the room exaggerated the many nicks and discolorations on its once statuesque legs, undoubtedly imposed years before by the gnawing clutches of a rambunctious puppy.

However, the chairs had not held up as well—wiggly, defying anyone of excessive poundage. Nearly ready for firewood, the maintenance man was consulted, hoping he could salvage a few.

The formerly-stylish suite had become a hodge-podge of disarray. Odd folding chairs flanked each side, an army of mismatched militia ready to serve and relied upon until finally, during one November election, a tax bill was passed allowing increased funding to the district.

It was announced that new equipment would soon be delivered, including a large conference table complete with matching chairs so comfortable it was feared people would doze off. The staff was delighted and, in a mood of celebration, decided the grandfather table should host its own retirement coffee. Cake crumbs were still being swept away as a large truck drove up to claim its donation.

"Got a table, ma'am?" a gravelly baritone voice questioned the school secretary.

"Yes, it's been part of our family for so long, but now we have a nice new one."

Ignoring the sentimentality, the man and his assistant tossed a covering over the table and lifted it into the van.

The secretary stood watching, almost as if bidding a fond farewell to an old friend. As the truck drove down the street and out of sight, she paused for just a minute, remembering all the companionship shared. Then she turned back into the room and gave the new conference table a pat of approval before returning to her day's work.

The manager of Relics and Remnants furniture store gestured his arm toward an area nearby. "Still a good-looking piece. It should sell quickly," the deliveryman commented. The two men agreed.

Raindrops accelerated into a thunderous storm on that afternoon in late March. A gust of wind blew open the door, giving a young couple no choice but to enter the store. Shaking the excess moisture from their jackets, it was obvious they were living on love rather than designer clothing. Their eyes darted anxiously across the room hoping to find a good bargain for their almost empty apartment.

"Oh, Jimmy, look over there at that table! It's so beautiful, from another era. It speaks to me."

Her partner took the bait. "So what is it saying?" he asked with a grin.

"It says it wants to come home with us. Let's buy it… please?"

"But Hon, that table's so big it'll overtake our entire pad and blow our budget for everything else."

Her voice became more assertive, and he realized she would not leave the store without her newfound treasure.

"It's a real antique with so much character. We'll just pay it out."

Her voice lowered, and she gave him a look that meant business.

"I really want it, Jim."

"But where are we going to put it?"

"I'll make it fit somehow. And I will give the most awesome dinner parties! We'll invite everyone we want to impress, and they'll rave. Jimmy, we need to buy it. It'll help our careers; you'll see."

Discussion over, Jimmy shook his head, both in agreement and in defeat. Extracting a credit card from his wallet, he reluctantly handed it to the salesman and softly said, "We'll take the table."

The love of his life smiled approvingly as she gently glided her fingertips across the table's worn cherrywood surface; then she turned to her Jim to brush his cheek with a kiss.

GO WEST—STILL GOOD ADVICE

L ife is uncertain.
　　Watch cowboy movies. The Good Guys always win.

In today's world, that's about as great as it gets. Well, maybe the sheriff is winged in the last scene, but as the credits roll, we're assured the bullet only grazed his buckskin jacket and he'll be nursed back to health by the beautiful native girl who suddenly appears out of nowhere.

Where she comes from and how our hero manages to avoid the barrage of gunfire doesn't really matter. What does count is the happy ending.

The story lines don't vary much, usually opening with suspicious-looking strangers loitering in the Golden Garter saloon. Right away you can see they're no good. As the bartender mops up the spilled whiskey, one character reaches under his coat. We know it's not to scratch his belly; he's fingering a Colt 45.

Trouble's a-brewin'. The door swings open and our fearless sheriff strides across the room with an "I dare you" look on his tough-guy face. He swaggers up to the bar and commands the gunslingers to get out of Dodge before sun up.

Gamblers crouch beneath their poker tables as the brazen barmaids (all of whom have a heart of gold) shriek in terror. Undisturbed, the player piano man pumps out "Sweet Clementine" though no one's listening.

Shielding themselves with a hostage, the outlaws shoot their way out through the swinging doors and jump on the horses conveniently saddled and waiting right there. Somehow they manage to hightail it up to a hidden canyon and wait to reappear when the bank opens the next morning.

In the following scene, the unfortunate teller (who pleads he has young'uns at home so they shouldn't shoot him) submits to the robbers' demands and opens the vault. With quivering hands he relinquishes the townsfolk's hard-earned cash. Excusing the small amount, he explains it was a lean year for crops.

The gang greedily grabs what they can before rushing out the back door. A posse chases after them. Bullets fly everywhere, and the bandits are cornered by the edge of town.

Again our courageous Sheriff confronts them. Though their faces are masked, the leader (with the meanest eyes) threatens to shoot. His trigger finger is itching. But before the lethal shot can be fired, a deputy sharpshooter, hiding on a rooftop, plugs the heart of the heartless, and the drama concludes. Remarkably all of this is accomplished without anyone's hat falling off.

The outlaws surrender, the money pouch is retrieved, and the Sheriff, as aforementioned, survives thanks to the slightly inebriated but nonetheless skilled hands of Doc Holliday.

In the closing scene, our Sheriff and his dark-eyed beauty almost kiss, there's sarsaparilla enough for everyone, the town is rescued once more and me—I ride off into the sunset content once again with a happy ending.

If only life could parallel a movie.

THE ENCHANTED GARDEN

A whisper of moisture touched my face, as if a gigantic bottle of champagne had just been uncorked in front of me and I was the designated recipient of its effervescence. Water spritzed my eyelids—an attempt to awaken me to a new morning. But this welcoming was only my interpretation, for the day had already begun, and the exhilaration I felt was emanating from a quartet of spigots placed in the pond into which I gazed.

The pool of water I refer to was no ordinary watering hole. It assuredly was not a cavernous puddle placed randomly in the center of two busy walkways. This pond had been meticulously crafted long ago by landscape architects well aware they needed to make a big splash on the far end of the famous Parisian Jardin des Tuileries: one of the most revered gardens in all of Europe. And this end, facing the Place de la Concorde, served as my beginning as I explored the glorious greenery that surrounded me.

The Tuileries derives its name from the abundance of clay found in its soil. This composition was perfect for making tiles ("tuiles" in French). In the sixteenth century, Catherine de Medici bought the area, which was adjacent to the Louvre, for her latest chateau. But even a queen's plans don't always work out, and after an assortment of kings named Louis and a couple of Napoleons moved in and out, the palace was deliberately burned to the ground during the Franco-Prussian War.

Being true to French drama, this was only one of many in a long series of invasions and riots, ransacks and slaughters, extending back for centuries. But all of this is history: today the gardens, minus the palace, have been transformed into an Eden of elegance. And I was commanding ownership, if only in my imagination, for a few treasured hours.

My throne was a green wooden chair which I'd been occupying alongside the pool. An attendant thoughtfully placed it there under the assumption that somebody like me would be in a pensive mood and drift into deep thought. Or, perhaps more likely, chat with a friend, or do nothing but watch the grass grow. Nice choices. The ladder-back slats did not particularly coincide with my contour, but no matter. I could crunch into an acceptable position without wondering where the nearest chiropractic office was located. Finally I rose from my chair, sensing the design had imprinted itself on my backside. Hopefully no one would notice as I walked through the hotel lobby. But before going back for a bath and dinner I had another stop to make.

As I walked along, a multitude of statuary stood imposingly on pedestals, as if each was a silent guardian of its designated spot on earth. I noted that each classical figure was draped correctly, in accordance with the historical volumes we were forced to read in high school. I allowed my mind to question these forgotten gods and heroes: Although forged in stone, could they ever play tricks on us by peering through those granite eyes to judge our appearance and behavior by ancient standards? What would they think of our decorum? Would they turn a cold shoulder or understand that people have never really changed? Only the draping of a tunic has. It's now called "haute couture" and comes at a price higher than the cost of a museum quality statue.

As I strolled among my mute observers, I felt hungry; the fresh air had stimulated an appetite and conveniently I spotted a makeshift cafe—a succession of tables and chairs set under a weathered awning that was once probably bright red. A very short woman, apparently the owner, stood directly in my path. Her eyes spoke the universal language. All options were out; I was to be her next guest. I was seated and handed a menu I could not read. The selections were in French; I functioned in English. Finally I managed to point to the soup l'oignon and my petite lady-friend quickly departed behind a group of trees three times her height. Presumably, somewhere in this forest was a real-life kitchen hidden from view, because moments later she reappeared carrying a small pot of rich broth simmering under a crouton covering. Cheesy too. (This comment refers to an ingredient—not the quality of the dish.)

I felt privileged. The trees were in full foliage and I was dining under a canopy of leaves. As I looked across the promenade, I thought of all the people, through countless decades, who had also enjoyed a meal embraced by similar beauty. Perhaps they opened wicker baskets prepared by servants and nibbled on paté exquisitely prepared by a chef de cuisine. Perhaps they sipped wine instead of diet Coke and raised cut glass goblets as they toasted each other with promises never kept.

I really don't want to know how their lives turned out because now I have license to create my own scenario, including visualizing those well-endowed gentlewomen who spilled down the front of their silk-embossed bosoms and dabbed discreetly with linen handkerchiefs because Kleenex had not yet been invented.

I savored the last of the soup and continued to scavenge the base of the bowl with my spoon, though I retrieved nothing. All had been devoured. It was time to resume my stroll. I started across an open field, lured by calliope music and the inviting lyrics of a soprano. As I approached, the woman's voice was diluted by the lilting laughter of children. To my delight, they were riding on a carousel ala Camelot. Each pony, painted and primed in medieval pageantry, was decorated with wooden carvings, all different, all equally handsome. Some horses rose on golden poles to the swell of the melodies. Others stood obediently in place as if they had been ordered to do so. All were chasing each other relentlessly, never to catch up but never to surrender their quest. The children, guarded by watchful parents, grabbed onto the animals' security straps as if they alone were taming the Wild West. Three turns around before home and nap time.

I thought of taking a ride myself; there were giant seashells with seats secured but, reluctantly, felt I'd look foolish. Thinking back now, I'm sorry that I forfeited that memory.

As I looked at the vast acreage I was now crossing, I was amazed to see that every shrub and tree was precisely the same height—not a renegade among them. Even if they had all been planted at the same time, it was remarkable that there was no variation due to differing soil composition or sunshine or rain. Every tree was identical in width and height. The bushes blended and flowed into one lineal extension. If this horticulture had been human, they would have been called The Radio City Rockettes. Could such an effect have come about naturally, or was it simply that when onlookers are slumbering a crew of elfin caretakers stealthily appear with clippers?

I stood on a pathway and looked both ways. Lithe joggers rushed by, while elderly couples moved gingerly as if their knees were particularly stiff that day. They barely conversed, as though the purpose for verbalizing had long since been erased by time. I glanced down at their hands, grasping each other's tightly, and knew this was all they needed to say.

Geometric designs of flowers were bedded down as carefully as newborn babes. Each stem protected by surrounding earth and had obviously been tended to oh so tenderly.

The colors harmonized in both swirls of monotone and a clever paradox of contrasts; a blanket of petals safely isolated from the danger of nearby trudging feet; all this beauty under the ambience of Parisian skies accented with dollops of whipped cream clouds overhead, while across a panorama, the Eiffel Tower stood sentry, as if to assure stability to all who were passing by, in the same way that protective parents do.

Everywhere I looked people were seemingly in love. As is to be expected: Paris and romance are synonyms. Perhaps there are magic vapors rising from the Seine or the scent of blossoms floating upwards along Le Boulevard. Perhaps the shadowy silhouettes cast by vintage street lamps provide a convenient cover for an unexpected kiss. Whatever—it's contagious, and I wish us all to know sweet moments of this ailment.

I felt more relaxed than I knew was possible; I had found what I needed, and I could leave the garden, radiant in the late afternoon sun, fulfilled. I walked up the stairs towards the Rue de Rivoli, passed the iron gates, and waited for the tiny figure on the road sign ahead to turn green. I moved quickly in the midst of a group of pedestrians. I had no desire to be flattened crossing the busy street. Safely on the other side, I glanced back over my shoulder and, surprisingly, heard myself sigh. And I still sigh whenever I recall that afternoon in the Tuileries garden. Those hours dusted with majesty.

I'm an American and content to be. Though the question remains: Would I interrupt my comfortable lifestyle, run up my Visa card, and fly for half a day crossing an ocean, just for a walk in the park (admittedly adding a croissant au chocolat to the deal)?

Two-second response: You betcha, Bebbé!

SOUP A L'OIGNON
(GRATINEED FRENCH ONION SOUP)

10 cups rich beef broth
2 tablespoons butter, melted
4 cups onions, thinly sliced
2 tablespoons flour
1 egg yolk
2 tablespoons lite cream
Salt and pepper to taste

Prepare beef broth; set aside. Saute onions in melted butter until golden. Sprinkle flour over sauteed onions; cook about 2 minutes. Add them to broth; simmer 15 minutes.

Remove 1 cup of broth from kettle; add egg yolk and cream to liquid. Mix well and pour into remaining beef broth. Season with salt and pepper, to taste. Simmer gently for 30 minutes.

Garnish with a small slice of bread, toasted or grilled with butter and sprinkled with shredded gruyere cheese.

– Serves 8

ALL APPLES ARE NOT CRABBY

Admittedly I have produce envy. As a lifelong resident of the Midwest and being a frequent shopper, it is usual to see bins of apples. Most all other seasonal fruit is shipped in from places that do not experience five-month winters.

Certainly, in the heat of July local farmers' markets proudly display berries and melons at stands around the city, but most of the year we get a bumper crop of apples. The University continually develops new species, putting us in competition with New York's "Big Apple" title. Call us the "Mid-sized Apple."

Apples cannot be categorized as a mere fruit, like the cumquat. Throughout history this round little object has been a major contributor, beginning with Eve's indulgence in the Garden of Eden. Succumbing to temptation, she took a major bite out of womanhood forever. But Adam got his name on our throats.

Snow White also indulged in a shiny red. One chomp and off she slumbered until awakened by a princely kiss. Hollywood's version of reality.

William Tell fell to the apple's lure, shooting the fruit off the top of his son's head. Just think, the Lone Ranger would ride in silence today if Will's arrow hadn't inspired that overture.

Apple blossoms are frequently used in weddings because, according to folklore, they represent love and fertility. In contrast, "You're full of applesauce," shouted at a wayward spouse, signals that the honeymoon is over.

Flying off to France, a Parisian waiter's pay would surely be garnished if he served a suckling pig without the garnish of an apple in its mouth.

Folklore has insisted "an apple a day keeps the doctor away." Though the American Medical Association has never substantiated this theory, perhaps someday Apple computer will tabulate data to corroborate.

Conversely, an apple for the teacher is reliable. Late homework, dozing in class, can be softened with a sweet gift. Every kid can give it a try.

Apple fragrance, from room freshener to a whiff of brandy, fills our lives. But nothing fills our bellies like apple pie, made, of course, by mom—if not yours, then somebody's somewhere. The great American contribution to great cuisine, apple pie with ice cream or cheddar cheese or just nibbled from the pan represents the best of desserts. Other countries have variations of tarts and flans but ours—deep-dish, warm from the oven with a hint of cinnamon—is everyone's favorite.

All this is making me hungry, so I will close with the assurance that you, dear reader, are the apple of my eye. I wish you success in whatever you pursue. Reach beyond the highest branch of the tallest apple tree and someday you just might find that pie in the sky.

My Favorite Four-Letter Word

Over the years I've been called many names—a selection of which inspire the imagination, and a few that require no imagination at all.

My favorite title contains only four letters. Unlike many in that category, it can be spoken aloud in a sanctuary and embroidered on a handkerchief. These four letters I speak of spell A-U-N-T, an honor bestowed upon select sisters.

This coveted crown includes Great Aunts who have matured into the third, even fourth generation, and close friends of the family. Those women having earned the privilege by remembering birthdays (and other life-shaping events) with gifts and perhaps baked goods.

An Aunt doesn't necessarily have to be born into the position. One can marry into it or simply acquire it in business by coaching an intern in the art of ladder climbing.

"You've been like an Aunt to me" is commonly exclaimed by the grateful trainee.

This qualifies as "Aunt Dome" and can be heard expressed in offices throughout our nation.

Marrying a man whose siblings have already produced children can be tricky. You automatically become a ready-made Aunt and are expected to sit through piano recitals and basketball games. Even when you're tired. It makes a good impression on your new family.

Aunts are back-up mothers. In the best of circumstances, an "Auntie" (which is the affectionate derivative) rarely disciplines. Even in a pinch the reprimand is gentle, not accusatory.

Aunts forgive easily and remember badly. Most are still young enough to recall with empathy their own impetuous mishaps and can be trusted to understand yours.

An Aunt skilled in her position usually finds the right words to say—or in some cases not to say, if silence is more appropriate.

Younger than a grandma, an Aunt is still able to get up off the floor after playing a board game. She can also climb up high bleachers to cheer on the team.

Often referred to as an "Ont," my Midwestern interpretation is sometimes confusing. By replacing one vowel with another, and dropping a "u" along the way, we now have a new pronunciation. I'll stay with what I know. Besides, "ont" eliminates the four-letter word club. And we can't allow that.

Oddly enough, another form of Aunts exists. While sharing the sane enunciation (except for the previously mentioned "ont" which we've already disposed of), these tiny black insects have no relationship to your mother's sister. Unless, of course, that woman leaves sticky candy wrappers around. Then the two converge.

Myriads of tiny bugs storm and swarm as they form an army intent on devouring the slightest microscopic morsel. Besides the obvious differentiation between ants and Aunts, the former invades and intrudes unwelcomed while Aunts are usually invited guests who frequently bring presents.

There's no "Aunt Day." Nor have I ever heard a song immortalizing "That Beautiful Bleached-blonde Auntie O' Mine."

Much has been written about mothers and fathers and elderly grandparents. The news occasionally has coverage of funny uncles—but that's a subject for another day.

So I thought it was about time to pay homage to the siblings of parents everywhere.

Nieces and nephews unite. You began life with, perhaps, a gift greater than a trust fund.

Certainly there's exceptions to all this. Sometimes it's geographical, sometimes conflicting attitudes. But when it is possible to be good together, it's great.

Aunt is a synonym for friend, to be tendered with care and gratitude. It's an opportunity for a would-be parent to nurture—without having to pay for the kid's orthodontia.

Enjoy.

Cousin Soupmeat

Oatmeal was bubbling in its pot, forming small craters that looked more like a science project than breakfast. But Mother didn't notice. She stood at the foot of the stairs hollering up to her children that they'd be late for school if they didn't get a move on.

Dad had already gulped his coffee and rushed off to an early morning meeting with prospective clients.

Everything about that nostalgic morning was ordinary. Even the dog was in his usual position under the table, eager to retrieve a bit of dropped bacon or any breakfast remnant (except, of course, the ominous oatmeal).

A routine day. Nothing more until the phone rang. Mother was startled. The phone never rang so early. Someone important must have died-or at least be in the hospital.

She moved swiftly, stretching the cord to its full length, grasping the receiver to her ear as she sat down to steady herself for what she feared would be shocking news.

My brother rushed towards her, anxious to overhear any information. But Mother's expression alone spoke volumes. Her eyes widened into enormous circles staring straight into space, much like the time a tiny grey mouse darted across the kitchen floor, running for refuge behind the refrigerator.

Sounds, too garbled to identify, emerged throughout the conversation. Finally, after what seemed like forever. Mother was able to respond. "Oh. my goodness, how exciting, he's coming here? Yes, we'll include the children. I'll call you back later, Ma." With that, she hung up the phone and took a deep breath before turning toward us.

"What is it?" I fairly shouted. My brother stood to the side with obvious disdain for what he considered over-reactive females. Ignoring his attitude. Mother spoke to us both.

"Children, there's someone I must tell you about. Someone you've never heard me speak of before." She cleared her throat to enunciate more clearly, "We have a cousin. He lives in New York and he's coming here to visit. His name is— well, that's just it. No one seems to know his real name; we've always called him 'Cousin Soupmeat.' It fit him so well."

She shrugged her shoulders as if to justify the decision and softly added, "It just stuck."

My brother was too astonished to reply but I burst into laughter. "'Soupmeat'? How could he be called something to eat? Does he have a sister 'Egg Noodles'?"

And with that, we couldn't control our giggling until Mother interrupted. "Now children, don't be disrespectful. I'll explain more tonight. Come eat your cereal and get ready for school."

She tried to sound firm, but I could see her lips tightening so a smile would not escape and give her secret away.

As we left the house that morning, we could hear Mother on the phone again—this time to Dad's office. "I know he's in a meeting, Miss Baxter, but please give my husband a message to call home as soon as possible. "No. don't be concerned, the children and I are fine, it's just—well, we've had unexpected news."

The school bus was in sight. We ran out the front door,

hoping Miss Baxter would get the word to Dad quickly. Cousin Soupmeat was headed West and time was of the essence.

It was hard to concentrate that day. Who cared about algebra with such excitement at home! During lunch, I was bursting to entice my friends, but thought it best to wait until I could embellish the news with dramatic details and throw in my own opinions for color.

That evening at the dinner table, Mother began her explanation, and we sat fascinated, even allowing our favorite beef barley soup to get cold. Dad, too. put down his spoon to listen. Apparently, Grandma had just received the "letter." It must have been written the day of departure but took three days (plus Sunday) to arrive all the way from New York, New York.

Mother paraphrased the message, "Dear family, I will be traveling through on my way to Nebraska and would enjoy spending a few hours with all of you. Arriving on the 4:30 bus Tuesday."

Mother gave Dad that double whammy expression she used whenever she wanted something and, as usual, he responded: "Okay. okay. I'll pick him up at the bus depot and take him to Grandma's."

Mother sat back, obviously pleased with herself. Everything was going as planned. She continued with additional details. Although many of the relatives dared to venture west from Ellis Island to the Midwest, Soupmeat was one cousin who had never travelled far from the East Coast; New York suited him just fine. He wasn't anyone's sibling, always being referred to as a "cousin once removed." But nobody could remember who he was removed from.

No matter, he was unquestionably a welcome part of

our family. There was a Mrs. Soupmeat. too, and several small Soupmeats, but they had never materialized—even in photographs. As no one had ever met them, their existence was only assumed. But who would contrive a story about having a wife and kids? Certainly not a man named after an entre!

Now we come to his intriguing title: it seems Soupmeat had earned his distinctive moniker by consuming vast and continuous amounts of his favorite food. In fact, it was the mainstay of his diet. Taking for granted that his wife threw in a few vegetables and a potato now and then, Soupmeat survived on soupmeat.

Of course, his children needed milk and shoes and someday perhaps orthodontia. So in order to support his family, he had taken a job selling men's belts to dime stores across Middle America. He didn't own an automobile: so for three weeks out of every month, he rode a Greyhound bus from city to city, stopping off wherever he spotted a potential outlet for his merchandise. Suspenders weren't popular with the younger crowd; belts were considered more stylish. So Soupmeat was able to sustain a modest income.

Over the years, he had built up a loyal clientele. Or maybe the appearance of an aging salesman lugging his well-battered sample case evoked compassion in prospective buyers. Mother didn't have the answer. But she insisted he was an honest businessman. Grandma had told her so. At the closing of each sale (along with a firm handshake), Soupmeat would enclose two business cards, in case one got misplaced, along with the invoice. Printed in capital letters was his pledge to stand behind each belt. If a buckle broke or the material got damaged, the owner was to contact him for an immediate refund—no questions asked. The only problem was that within a day, Soupmeat would travel to another part of the country and was conveniently impossible to find.

At first, my father shook his head in feigned disbelief, but then he began to laugh, which made it okay for his children to laugh, too. Mother could not have made all of this up. Her imagination wasn't that vivid. I couldn't wait for tomorrow to arrive.

I raced from the bus after a restless day at school to bang open the door and nearly trip over the line-up of boxes. Grandma had given detailed instructions: bring the large coffee carafe, an extra roasting pan, the ivory tablecloth with matching napkins, and oh, please don't forget, some fresh flowers. Mother complied, setting each item out individually for her children to help load into the car.

The anxiety in her voice was evident. "You can put the extra container in the back seat if the trunk is filled. The three of us can squeeze into the front. Dad just called from the bus terminal They're on their way.

Soon we, too, were on our way to Grandmother's house, eager to bring our contributions. It was the beginning of rush hour. Mother took every side street in hopes of avoiding traffic. She also rolled through a few stop signs, telling us that when we learned to drive we shouldn't do what she just did.

It was a relief to finally arrive and see that ours was the first car in the driveway

"Hurry, children!" Mother shouted as she grabbed the nearest container and rushed ahead to open the front door. As I entered, struggling to balance a carton of candlesticks, I stopped, too stunned to proceed.

Perhaps it was the glistening chandelier reflecting a glow on the recently cleaned windows that made the small vestibule respond with a welcoming warmth. The wooden bench that guests sat on to pull off their winter boots had been given a rubdown with lemony-scented polish. A stack of magazines, turning yellow with age, were neatly piled alongside. The three umbrellas in the copper metal stand stood upright, ready to snap open in salute.

I proceeded to enter a living room I'd never seen before. There, positioned on carpeting that still bore the imprint of a vacuum cleaner, was the sectional sofa; pillows of blue and purple and green plumped in formation along the back of the couch. Grandma had always kept her prized upholstery covered—hidden away under a plastic covering much as if it were a gigantic slab of beef packaged for the freezer. Tonight, at long last, it got air time!

Both the sofa and I needed to breathe. As I inhaled, aromas too wonderful to forget floated in from the kitchen. I rushed towards this gateway to happiness and saw my grandmother scurrying across the room, critiquing the culinary skills of my two aunts.

"Molly, be sure to heat the milk and butter before you add them to the mashed potatoes."

"Yes. Ma, I know that, Ma," replied her indignant daughter.

But Grandma was oblivious to any inflection, continuing to give commands to anyone who would listen. This usually docile little lady, who had patiently taught me to knit and purl and play chopsticks on the piano, had suddenly morphed into a Queen Bee, soaring—and roaring—over her collective workers.

Mother and I were instructed to finish setting the table.

Wine glasses were to be shined with a soft towel until they reflected the light, I thought it was a silly task. The glasses would soon be filled, obliterating my effort. But I dared not object and afterwards folded each napkin to stand alongside. I was about to step back to admire my artistry when someone shouted, "God, they're here already!"

I stared at the ensemble of women. In unison, they untied their aprons, patted their hair, ran to their purses to search for a lipstick, while reassuring each other they looked just fine.

We heard the front door open. I gave my brother a shove so that I could get in front of him and catch a first glimpse of this mystery guest. My father entered, calling out, "Hello, we're here!" to everyone in the house. And the house responded with a thunderous ovation of shoes filled with the feet of eager relatives rushing forward. Soupmeat, the myth and the man, was actually here! No longer an intriguing story, no longer the amusing anecdote who had kept my family in awe, he had actually materialized, and I was about to meet him.

I can picture him as clearly today as I did on that impressive evening. I don't know what I expected in my youthful mind—at the very least, perhaps, a slayer of dragons. But in reality, I saw a round-shouldered, middle-aged man who needed a shave. I glanced at the bulging suitcase he'd been lugging, which explained his posture. Wisps of graying hair sprang capriciously over his balding head. His ample belly had crossed the threshold before the rest of him, followed soon after by scuffed brown oxfords that revealed the journey of a man who had trudged thousands upon thousands of miles.

Finally, I reached his face. Ordinary. But there was something I liked about it. His skin looked smooth under the stubble of a day's beard. But I excused that. After all, he'd just disembarked from a lengthy bus trip. His eyes, too, showed the weariness of travel. They were dark and the lids were heavy from fatigue. But when he smiled his eyes brightened, giving his whole presence a warmth, and I smiled, too.

Each aunt burrowed her way through, attempting to outshine her competition with syrupy words of welcome. "So nice to see you, Soupmeat," Aunt Becky cooed as Molly pushed in front to plant a quick kiss on his cheek. But Grandma breezed in like a shooting star. After all, it was her house and her dinner to enjoy.

"Hello, cousin." She extended her hands to grasp his as they both exchanged polite lies about how neither had aged a day since they last met.

The entourage of well wishers guided their guest to the sofa and tossed the obtrusive pillows aside so he could sit down. My brother and I were then introduced. He received a pat on the head and I got a pinch on the cheek, along with the prediction that someday I'd grow up to be pretty.

Dad interceded, "How about a good Schnapps, Scotch, or Bourbon? What'll it be?" His offer was strategically timed, fearing I would react to such a questionable compliment. Grandma gave my mother a look that needed no words, and the two women turned towards the kitchen, followed obediently by the aunts. My father then suggested, 'Why don't you children help with dinner?' The tone of his voice allowed us no option as we, too, left the men alone to enjoy their drink.

The kitchen was warm. The heat emitted by the oven made me uncomfortable, and I immediately removed my sweater, hoping no one would notice the stain on my blouse which had appeared on it earlier when I nipped a chunk of strudel.

"'Stand out of the way, children. Here's celery and carrot sticks. Go put them on a plate " Grandma instructed. The women stayed in separate traffic lanes, dashing around, each with an assignment, each on a time schedule.

I could hear the front door opening as various relatives entered with boisterous greetings of welcome: uncles cousins, all anxious to meet the man with the curious title.

Dinner was about to be served. Grandma approached her oversized metal stove—the one so reminiscent of an artist's impression on a holiday greeting card. That workhorse of appliances represented all that was wholesome and wonderful to come home to. She extended her right hand and with one forceful yank pulled open the heavy oven door. Wearing a quilted asbestos glove that reached halfway up her short arm, she withdrew the rack supporting an enormous cast iron roaster. The lid opened as all of us who were privileged to witness stood in silent awe. There, nestled within the cavity, was the coveted cuisine: fat juicy morsels of Soupmeat. Mountains of obviously soft and tender meat were clinging together in a sea of simmering sauce, browned to perfection, appearing almost golden as the late afternoon sunbeams streamed through the kitchen windows. Slices of carrots and translucent onion rings bobbled here and there, attempting to maneuver any area allowed by the dominating beef.

If only the aroma could be bottled and sold, I thought, it would compete with the finest fragrance. But such a scent could never actually be captured. It was a fleeting moment of intoxication reserved only for one's memory. Grandma reached for her blue clina dinner bell, and the tinkling crystals within drew everyone to the table.

After all were seated, a large tureen was place at the head of the table. Soup was to be the first course. Displaying the dexterity of a tennis pro. Mother angled her right wrist grasping a ladle to pour two scoops of broth into each bowl. It then became my job to add a garnishment of parsley as the guests relayed each serving along the table, much like a fire brigade, only slower.

When everyone had been served, Grandma gave a short blessing and soon the clicking of spoons chimed in unison. It was really quite rhythmic, along with an occasional slurping sound coming from the direction of my brother.

A farmers' market of salad greens, tossed with crimson tomato slices mingled with curlicues of sweet peppers, were placed on each end of the table. Everyone was to help themselves. Valleys of mashed potatoes, oozing with streaks of melting butter, arrived in containers almost too heavy to lift. The aroma of warm bread, so fresh it resisted slicing, was positioned near cut-glass bowls of homemade strawberry preserves But these were only the escorts to the star of the show.

At Grandma's beckoning, my father left his chair to follow her into the kitchen. This was to be his reward for rushing from his office early to get to the bus terminal on time. Chatter around the table continued, but no one was really paying attention to anyone else. It was obvious that everybody was eavesdropping, straining to hear the conversation in the adjacent room. We heard sounds; Grandma's voice was dictatorial, Father's conciliatory.

And then it happened. Beaming as though he was

escorting the Royal Heir to the throne, my father appeared in the doorway with a dazzling display. As if on cue, everyone inhaled simultaneously. For there, on a recently polished silver platter, in all its glory, was Grandma's famous soupmeat. She had outdone herself. A dinner created in honor of the man who bore its name.

It was only proper that he be served first. With the accuracy of a triumphant warrior, Soupmeat speared the large serving fork into three, maybe four, hunks of meat, one after the other, and placed them on his plate, followed by a sloshing of au jus from a tablespoon held in his left hand—all this activity while emanating a sound similar to multiple tires deflating.

The platter and everything else was then shared with the rest of the ravenous. "Pass the bread so I can mop up the gravy" and "ready for refills" were repeated throughout the meal. My grandmother beamed but did not get up from her chair. Her work was done. She sat entitled, basking in compliments and multiple helpings.

After some time, when everyone insisted they couldn't swallow another bite, a tray of pastries and coffee was served. With diligence and determination, the desserts were consumed despite protests of regret. Grandma then asked for kitchen volunteers Many of us quickly disappeared to the comfort of the living room. Soupmeat dived into the center of the couch just where the two cushions submerged. But it didn't seem to annoy him. Perhaps all those hours navigating worn bus padding had given him an implacable posterior. His attention turned to an audience of wide-eyed youngsters sprawled on the floor before him.

"Tell us your adventures on the bus!" squealed the oldest. The others were quick to agree. "Yes, yes, we want to hear everything."

"Everything? Well, I'll tell you the best stories I can," replied Soupmeat. We could see the amusement in his eyes. He was playing a game with us but it was done in such good humor we pretended to believe what he pretended had happened. And so he continued on about the woman who brought a chicken along for the ride. He laughed. "Most people pack a chicken sandwich, but she had the real thing!" He continued joking about the fellow who sat next to him all the way to Milwaukee. "Whenever I spoke to him, he'd sing his reply. It wasn't so bad at first, but after awhile I knew all the lyrics."

As he continued talking, and we got to know this character who had whisked into our lives, we became new old friends.

Now it was our turn to giggle. Soupmeat continued to regale us with tales so preposterous they sounded as though he was making them up as he went along. Or perhaps, they were originally concocted to entertain those rumored children he had left behind.

When he could go no further, when the exaggeration became too large even for his gullible admirers, Soupmeat reached for his loyal companion: a well-worn sample case. Bruised from being tossed on too many luggage racks, it remained upright, ready to serve its owner.

The tarnished hinges still snapped to attention as he opened the lid, and he allowed each of us to withdraw and examine a belt of choice. Some were narrow, while others were wirier, and came in the customer's choice of brown or black. One style was braided elastic, easy to loosen after a big meal. Our fingers slid easily over the slippery leather. "Why does this feel so funny?' asked my brother. Soupmeat hesitated and then replied quietly, "It's … ah … man-made, son."

"You mean it's synthetic, like plastic," quipped one of the older boys. Soupmeat just shrugged and diverted our attention to a buckle imprinted with a horse. Supposedly, it was Buffalo Bill's stallion, but, again, he wouldn't verity the origin.

Authenticity didn't matter. It was such an adventure to explore the entire case. Careful to avoid damaging the merchandise, we realized we could not leave any evidence we'd ever been there. One by one, a belt was wound back into its snake-like coil and placed in the previous pattern. Soupmeat explained this was necessary for his sales pitch. He knew just which item to introduce when a customer was losing interest. It was all in the timing to close the deal. For example, the horse with the saddle stitching was his biggest seller in the Dakotas, so that one was to stay in front.

I wanted to help. I grabbed a napkin from the dining room table, hoping to brighten the dingy metal buckles. But Cousin Soupmeat explained that the buckles were supposed to have an "antique patina." None of us knew what that was but we nodded in agreement anyhow.

I stopped my shining and watched as he extended his arms to close the lid and, with the flutter of both thumbs, snapped the latches tight. It was a quick, clicking sound signaling the case of curiosities was closed.

Just as abruptly. Mother reminded us it was a school night and time to leave. We started to object but our guest interrupted saying that he, too, had a bus to catch.

With that announcement, Soupmeat rose from the couch, brushed off his jacket as though telling remnants of dinner had infiltrated the fabric, and began the ritual of thank-yous and good-byes. Ceremoniously, he kissed cheeks of the ladies and foreheads of everyone much shorter. The men and boys over twelve got a pumping handshake, except for my father, who was driving him back downtown to catch his late evening bus.

I stood near the door, suddenly too shy to speak, although there was so much I wanted to say. I wanted to tell him how fun it was to meet him—to even know he existed—and that I'd surely tell all my friends about tonight and they would envy me forever.

But none of these words came out. I just stood there, struck silent. But oddly enough, I sensed that Cousin Soupmeat caught the message. He stopped and smiled at me for an extra minute and filled our awkward farewell with a gentle ruffling of my hair and a wink too quick for the others to catch.

We were never to see Cousin Soupmeat again. The next morning my father reported he'd taken him to the terminal and watched as he boarded the express to Omaha. This workworn peddler, whose name nobody knew or had even bothered to ask, had charmed a roomful of strangers just by being so delightfully ordinary.

Regrettably, he never came back to visit, and no one seems to know what happened to him. But he still remains vivid to me. The stories of his encounters, the characters he described, and the imaginary customers who wore his belts fill those memories with laughter.

I picture him as he was so long ago—a life-weary optimist still grasping at the dream that success was one bus ride away. A good man—far more genuine than the "leather" belts he tried to hustle.

Minneapolis and Indianapolis Are Not the Twin Cities

One would imagine, in this age of enlightened communication, that two American cities are familiar to almost everybody over the age of twelve.

This may be true with New York and L.A., but it doesn't hold water in the land of ten thousand lakes or a mid-sized metro in Indiana.

Contrary to the belief of many, Minneapolis and Indianapolis are not the "Twin Cities."

It never ceases to astound me that whenever I travel, this confusion exists among so many of the people I meet.

Being of a sociable nature and believing that time passes more quickly when I don't keep looking at my watch, I often open conversations with fellow travelers.

"So where are you from?" is the usual ice-breaker.

They answer; I reply with a standard nicety and wait for their response. I watch their expression as I say, "Minneapolis."

Eyebrows raise and heads nod as though my reply needs confirmation because few have met an honest-to-goodness Minnesotan. Exhibit A from the land of the Vikings.

Grappling for a response they exclaim, "Oh, the Twin Cities—Minneapolis and Indianapolis!"

I pause for dramatic effect. Then I speak in a whispered tone so they must listen intently.

"No, Indianapolis is in Indiana, a thousand miles from Minnesota. It would be geographically, if not structurally, impossible for these two cities to merge. Twins, in every form, are connected together. Whether it involves two people who are siblings or real estate territory, they must be linked to one another. In this case, St. Paul is the twin to Minneapolis."

I continue, "The two cities are divided by 'Ole Man River. There are several bridges connecting the two metros making it possible to be in two places at nearly the same time. St. Paul is the older city and was chosen to be the capitol. Minneapolis grabbed the university. Everybody was happy, except for Stillwater, a small community nearby which got stuck with the state prison. But that's a story for another day."

I've noticed people feel a need to rhyme. It does give a sense of tidiness. This is good in a "June Moon" lyric. But cities can be named for whatever the developers choose: in honor of the guy who chopped down the first tree to create a pathway, or for some philanthropist who donated the initial money to build Main Street.

Minneapolis means "city on the water." It combines the Native American Dakota word for water with the ancient Greek "polis" meaning city. St. Paul is a well-known religious tribute.

I am not responsible for Indianapolis.

My fellow travelers could not leave it here. After giving them the geography lesson they slept through in school, I answer questions about our infamous winters.

To accentuate their point more vividly, their queries are usually accompanied by a broad shiver which includes draping their arms around their shoulders to demonstrate a sudden chill.

"No, it does not snow in July," I reply with a smile.

There is a temptation to tease their apprehension with trigger words like "wind chill" and "frozen tundra" and "below zero." But unless I'm in a frisky mood, I restrain, preferring to turn the conversational toward our winter sports, stylish clothing, and the enjoyment of a delicious beef stew eaten by a fireplace.

Knowing we will never meet again, I talk fast about the products of major corporations in the city, beginning with my personal favorites: 3M's sticky notes and Betty Crocker's chocolate fudge cake mix.

But it is not enough. I see their interest is waning as they glance behind me looking for a door to anywhere. I have only a minute to become memorable, to send them home eager to educate themselves with a map of the contiguous forty-eight states.

I resort to a visual. On a gentle summer's day, when lake waters reflect a cloudless sky and small ducks on the beach play follow the leader, I proudly think to myself "Minneapolis, there's no place prettier!"

As they walk away I add, "St. Paul's nice, too!"

CRAZY RUTHIE

Her name was Ruth. But everyone referred to her as "Crazy Ruthie," a title well earned. For Ruthie's behavior was determined by her own rules of conduct. It was not that she was unaware of proper behavior. She just didn't care.

"Crazy Ruthie" wasn't crazy in the clinical sense. She had simply established (at the earliest age) an ardent desire to fly by the light of the moon, and no reprimand from two conservative parents could coax her from the glow of freedom back to planet Earth. She viewed her behavior as acceptable as long as (in her opinion) no one else got hurt.

Ruthie was not mean-spirited. Defiant and self-absorbed perhaps, but her heart was well intentioned.

Ruth's journey began as the "throw-away" child of an unknown father and an irresponsible mother. Apparently the result of her many "one nighters."

Her head full of raven hair, coal-black eyes, and olive complexion indicated a blending of cultures.

It did not matter to the couple eager to adopt the baby girl. Longing for a child they couldn't conceive, they were beyond delighted when the adoption agency called Jenny and John to come meet their newborn.

Perhaps, even at their first introduction, there was a forewarning. The baby stared at them and began to cry, as if she was sensing they would approach life on different terms.

"Where are you taking me? I did not give you permission." Looking back, it might have been an ominous prediction.

Jenny picked her up, but the screaming intensified. "You have no right to control my future."

Unexplainable intuition emerged from a pink-blanketed baby destined to enter a home in which she would never be happy.

Allowing for her outbursts of temper, as they would for the remainder of their lives, the joyful new parents signed the necessary papers pledging their loyalty and scooped the little girl into their arms for the journey home to her awaiting nursery.

It was decided to name the baby "Ruth" in honor of a long deceased grandmother. No one in the entire family could recall much about the woman since she had emigrated from Eastern Europe speaking no English, but all agreed she'd been a "good soul" and was certainly entitled to a namesake.

Little Ruthie, of course, spoke no English either, but her presence was profoundly heard. A restless baby who instinctively seemed to defy routine, Ruthie preferred to stay awake at night and sleep into the morning.

Her eating pattern was similarly contrary, demanding sweets before she would swallow a vegetable.

Jenny and John refused to acknowledge this disobedience, preferring to attribute it all to "spunkiness."

From an early age, Ruth knew she was onto something. Her obstinacy was profitable, a direct payoff for getting it all her way. Her frustrated parents, inexperienced and confused, found the path of least resistance to be the most peaceful. Ruth had set in stone her dominance.

Within a few years the nursery could not contain her.

As soon as she was able to put one foot in front of the other, she headed toward the door to freedom. Whatever was out there looked better than what was inside. Whether it was chasing the scattering leaves cast from an autumnal breeze or the playful capture of a neighbor's puppy, Ruth was intent on her pursuit.

Huffing and puffing closely behind was her "Nanny du jour," red-faced and breathless, trying to keep up. This was of no concern to Ruthie, nor did she even glance back because soon there would be a new Nanny. And another one after that. For as much as Jenny wanted a child, she had not anticipated the change in her lifestyle.

It had seemed so easy listening to sweet anecdotes her friends told of their children and viewing the pictures of happy birthday parties. A smart woman, it nonetheless did not occur to Jenny that motherhood was a full-time job, one that would interfere with her other nearly full-time occupation of being a patron of the arts. For much of her marriage, Jenny had been enrolled in community projects, helping raise money for, as she put it, "the less fortunate." She had worked diligently, establishing a fine reputation which she had no intention of trading for an afternoon pushing a swing at the park playground.

This social activity, along with her husband's executive position, required frequent dinner engagements for both of them, leaving their daughter to eat with whoever was hired for the night.

Her parents' absence fit well with her attitude. "Ruthie's Rules," as the family jokingly referred to them, grew as she did. No longer did she run away when an exuberant mood enticed her. In its place she simply set her own elastic margins.

Either a lack of foresight, or perhaps her quest for calm, influenced Jenny's decision to allow Ruthie such latitude. She convinced John to be equally lenient; it seemed a fair trade-off for keeping their defiant daughter agreeable.

Clothing worn during the week was tossed on the floor, making it difficult to step through the room. Bags of snacks and half-emptied bottles of soda were left on her nightstand until someone (other than Ruthie) tidied up.

Occasionally when a relative came visiting, words of reprimand were spoken. Ruthie responded silently, exhibiting her anger by gesturing a kick towards the ankles of her critic. Instead of a reprimand, Jenny covered her embarrassment with nervous laughter and quickly changed the subject.

School was a different matter. Despite excuses for tardiness or neglecting homework, Ruthie did comply. After her first threat of expulsion, she never again tried smoking in the girls' lavatory. Quite to everyone's amazement, she was a good student, displaying a talent in art. How she inherited this gift was a mystery of genetics but by her teens, she showed a great ability—if it could be corralled with discipline.

Ruthie was smart and attractive in her own unique way. With long, straight hair the color of ebony, her dark eyes were intense, tiger-like, quick to calculate everyone's every movement. Her features were sharp, with high cheekbones and a skin tone of burnished bronze. Slender and lithe, she had style. When she entered a room people noticed.

There was no question about a career. After high school she applied, and was accepted, to a prestigious art school. Her talent was exceptional. But, once again, Ruthie's lack of self-control interfered. By this time she had discovered a new avocation—young men. With the stamina of youth and the audacity of the indulged, she was frequently in pursuit, no longer for a lost puppy but for any fellow who pleased her. And most of them did. The joke went around school about Ruthie's chasing her man of the hour up a flight of stairs to be caught for a kiss on the landing. Which led many male students, who could not outrun her, to hide in the elevator.

Despite her aggressiveness, her paintings represented her well. She was asked to display her work both on campus and at galleries around town. It was at one of these showings that she met her first husband.

Louis was also an artist, a promising sculptor with an eye for anything creative, which included our Ruthie. Since there were no stairs to catch him on, she simply said "Yes" to his late-night proposal.

Louis was older but not wiser, so the two had much in common besides their physical attraction. For he decreed his own similar boundaries, whatever suited him at the moment.

His small apartment in Greenwich Village was a combination home and studio. It was by chance he'd accepted a friend's invitation to come in town for that fateful gallery show where it all began. Ruthie took one glance at the guy with prematurely gray hair and was entranced. She called him her "Silver Fox," and indeed he was just that. Louis charmed the girl who had parents wealthy enough to finance his career and sponsor his exhibits. It was a perfect pairing; he wanted money, and she wanted to escape from her parents.

Louis stayed around long enough to captivate Ruthie and his budding reputation in the art world impressed Jenny and John. But before they would support their nineteen-year-old daughter moving to New York, John insisted the couple get married.

"It would only be proper," he determined.

From her many years doing charity galas, Jenny was an experienced event planner; putting together a wedding was easy. Not a large celebration, just art friends and, of course, both families.

Ruthie chose a designer gown for the ceremony, changing into another "label" dress for dancing. Louis' mother happened to walk into the bride's room after her new daughter-in-law had left. After seeing the exquisite hand-made gown tossed carelessly on the floor (as was Ruthie's habit), she cried out in anguish, "Oh my God, what has my son gotten himself into!"

Those nearby looked away, too embarrassed to respond.

With the nuptials over, Ruthie convinced her parents that she and Louis needed to honeymoon in Italy (presumably to study the Great Masters). On an all-expense paid trip, they spent their first summer in Florence before settling into Louis' village apartment. It was the best time either had ever known. Ruthie set up her easel in one corner while her husband chiseled away. Louis hired an agent and, through John's contacts, was booked for impressive gallery showings.

The entire family was relieved that Ruthie finally had become a responsible adult. She had no choice because soon there was a baby. And another the next year.

Although Louis had sold much of his work and was achieving national recognition, commission checks were inconsistent and Ruthie could only profit sporadically between child care. They had moved into a small apartment without extra space for a studio. That meant another rental for their work. Although they weren't the proverbial "starving artists," the monthly checks from John helped. But it wasn't a long-term solution. Reluctantly, they realized the only sensible path would be for Louis to give up sculpting and come into the family business. There was a good opportunity at John's office with the guarantee for a secure and comfortable lifestyle.

But this reality was hard to accept. For months they searched for alternatives, objecting vehemently to relinquishing their freedom. But the procrastination only reinforced John's ultimatum to either come home and work at his company or the monthly checks would stop. Options were over. They had two children to feed.

For the first time, Ruthie acquiesced, and the family closed their apartment and their studio and moved back to Ruthie's hometown. There they bought a large traditional home with a thirty-year mortgage within walking distance of her parents' house—and their constant observation.

Louis was thrust into an executive position in a business about which he knew little and cared less. Life continued down a straitjacket course: two people encased in, what seemed to them, an inescapable monotony.

Even with a steady income, Ruthie was continually overdrawn. Impulsive spending was her release from boredom. Louis drew a generous salary, far more than he contributed, although he tried hard, forcing himself to wear a conservative suit and going to work every day. Plummeting an artist into the world of progress reports and statistical data was difficult. He, too, indulged himself financially as a release from stress.

Neither parent stopped to foresee that small girls grow up and need college.

Ruthie felt plastered into a mold, and she desperately searched for an escape before the walls hardened around her. She found it, quite by accident. With her artistic background, she decided to decorate the house. It was an older place, but the spacious rooms had potential. It would be an interesting project. Louis agreed on her choice of Scandinavian Modern: sleek, with good lines.

Ruthie checked out showrooms, finally settling on one with an extensive inventory. It also included the best looking sales manager, for he, too, had good lines. Erik was a towering man with a brush of blond hair and an athletic physique. Ruthie imagined that the store used him in advertisements, for his rugged features were remarkable. More than that, his eyes were a shade of green she had never before seen on any palette. If money could buy happiness, hers did that day.

Ruthie loitered the first afternoon pretending to need advice on each piece of furniture, finally leaving Erik's company only because she had to pick up her children at daycare. In the future, she would hire a sitter who could drive.

Erik was impressed with the spirited Ruthie. She certainly looked different, more exotic, than the women he was accustomed to. The two met at the store several times, then talked over long lunches which eventually became late afternoon "cocktails" at Erik's apartment.

Ruthie, experienced at bending the truth, told Louis she was taking a pottery class and the instructor kept her late. She insisted. He believed her. But after months of excuses he became suspicious when she never brought home a single vase. Of the so-called "pots," the only thing she was throwing was a line of deceit.

The inevitable happened. Louis resigned his position with John's company and, with much relief, got into his sports car and drove back to New York, vowing to never leave again. He eventually did chisel his way to a fine reputation.

Ruthie and Erik married for a remarkably short time. He suddenly was offered a position in the home office and, without informing Ruthie, departed for North Carolina. She never heard from him again—except through his lawyer.

That left her with a house full of used Scandinavian-style furniture, two little kids and inconsistent family maintenance as Louis' income was sporadic and clients couldn't be identified. His checks did not come regularly because he knew John would take over.

Ruthie's ordeal with domesticity was finished. She sold the house (including the now contemptuous furnishings) and moved with her daughters to Los Angeles. Between money from the home and John's monthly checks, she rented a small apartment.

A few years passed. Presumably the girls were cared for properly. Louis had since remarried and focused on his new family, so Ruthie remained a single parent.

Life could have been on a straight course, but her restless spirit drove her off track. That's exactly what happened. Ruthie began to race cars. She had always enjoyed exceeding speed limits, even as a teen driving her mother's Buick. Now with her children in school, she had all day to practice on county roads. But it was not enough. Ruthie wanted to perfect her technique, so she inquired around to find which bar the professional racers frequented. It was easy, and initial conversations developed into friendships. Soon Ruthie was, literally, in the driver's seat. Learning from experts, she began racing competitively. Eventually developing an impressive reputation, she was asked to be a stunt driver in an Elvis Presley movie, impersonating the lead actress in a drag car race (of which Elvis won, of course!).

Although Ruthie defied maturing, the years compounded for everyone else, including Jenny and John. Concerned about their daughter's lifestyle, they had been sending monthly checks to assure their granddaughters were well cared for. Now elderly and ill, it was becoming more serious. Without Ruthie's knowledge, they established a long-term financial arrangement, airtight and non-negotiable. Not too generous but adequate security. This way the young girls would at least have an income and their mother would not be on the street, for they feared what desperate acts she would resort to if she was.

Angry with the restrictions of her inheritance, Ruthie threw all her energy into drag racing, becoming so proficient she earned the admiration of the other female drivers. They spent their days competing and their nights outdrinking one another.

Word got out that one of the pack, a loudmouth who couldn't control his alcohol, had smashed his race car, which was sponsored by a social club in Santa Monica. He survived but was abruptly fired. Ruthie immediately contacted the club's owner and asked to replace him.

She concocted an idea he couldn't refuse, offering to be a vocalist there on weekends. With her usual audacity and the help of an experienced accompanist who could hide her mistakes, she pulled off the audition and was hired to sing two nights a week gratis in exchange for the club's sponsoring her car in competitive races.

Ruthie managed to transform her appearance from a grease-stained, jump-suited racer into a sleek and sultry vocalist, a metamorphosis in borrowed black satin with "jewels" from Walmart.

Although she would never be signed by a label, Ruthie's voice was good enough, a husky alto, to bring in a crowd. When she couldn't hit a note, she spoke the lyrics with adequate expression to get her through, especially those laments of love on the rocks. Far more important, it got her the sponsorship she wanted.

The upcoming racing schedule was crowded with opportunities to choose from. The one that appealed to her most was the Lowriders of Chicano Culture in Southwest New Mexico. She could easily race and still return in time for her weekend gig.

Ruthie entered the competition and, perhaps stimulated by the cheers of the crowd, drove exceptionally well that day. Deciding to reward herself with a cold beer, she entered the nearest bar where she quickly collided with José, a soon-to-be third husband.

Seeing friends sitting across the room, Ruthie walked towards them when, in the dim light, she nearly tripped over a protruding foot stuck obtrusively in her path.

"What the f---, you could have killed me!"

"Is that the way you say hello?" he said, a grin brightening his face.

"I could've said more, but I went easy on you!"

The man who belonged to the foot continued smiling and staring at her.

"I'm José. Can I apologize with a drink?"

Ruthie liked his easy manner and joined him for the remainder of the night.

José Martinez was a middle-aged rancher who had moved to Durango, Colorado, from his native Mexico. He raised goats, along with a small herd of sheep, managing to eke out a decent living. A short, rather squat man whose ruddy complexion resulted from years of sun exposure, he was nonetheless sufficiently attractive to follow her back to L.A. and move in. He soon proposed; she accepted and even agreed to move to Durango. Her daughters, now grown, remained in California.

The house was modest but suited the needs of a rancher. Ruthie cooked and infrequently helped care for the animals. A neighbor woman came in each day to clean and do chores, which gave Ruthie the opportunity to paint the sprawling scenery surrounding her. The beauty of the land inspired her, and before her first anniversary she had produced enough work to show at a nearby gallery (actually on the walls of the local poolroom adjacent to the best bar in town).

The reviews were surprisingly encouraging, rewarding Ruthie with new income and resurging her interest in art.

But, as was her pattern, Ruthie twisted an asset into a liability, becoming dissatisfied with only local attention. Assuming her work was worthy of praise by prominent curators from upscale galleries in Los Angeles, she packed her supplies, waved good-bye to Durango, and told José he could follow her if he wanted to. He did not. But they never bothered to divorce.

What had been remarkable in a small Colorado community soon became overlooked in a cosmopolitan city, especially one in which creativity flourished.

Ruthie's art was displayed in limited venues, such as retail spaces and her own apartment. Instead of using oils, she began experimenting in pencil, black and gray geometric designs. Detailed to the point of intricacy, her work appealed to only a limited clientele.

Friends from her race driving years suggested she paint similar designs on their hubcaps. They would pay her and she, in turn, would receive free advertising. Ruthie grabbed the suggestion and began a new career decorating the hubcaps of race cars.

Her unique reputation quickly expanded to members of motorcycle clubs. Although she couldn't add artwork to their vehicles, she was accepted as one of the gang. They taught her to ride; she taught them to drink, although they didn't need much training.

This was to be the final chapter of Ruthie's life: riding against the wind on a Harley Davidson. Her lustrous dark hair of long ago was now grayed with the years, disclosing a face saturated with life's excesses.

Her artistic work—her many paintings, including the emblazoned flourishes on hubcaps—seems to have disappeared, perhaps hiding to be rediscovered by another flamboyant soul. Realistically a few of Ruthie's creations might yet exist, unbeknownst to the owner and used as decoration to cover a stained wall.

Her life remains a puzzle with major pieces missing, leaving questions to be answered by each individual, for everyone will interpret differently.

Here we confront the age-old dilemma of "heredity versus environment." Perhaps, just perhaps, if her birth parents had kept her, allowing Ruthie's free spirit to thrive unconditionally, she would have been less rebellious. What compelled her to break all norms to satisfy herself? Why was the need insatiable?

Jenny and John had the best of intentions but they could not, would not, extend themselves beyond their own margins of conduct. And the pressure of their conformity was simply too restrictive for their undisciplined daughter.

Throughout her unorthodox life, Ruthie constantly chose the side roads, forever taking detours in search of acceptance, being content with less than what she could have been, compromising the promise of her potential.

How different Ruth could have been. And how much easier it would have been for the people in her life who, in spite of all she became, tried to love her.

Inn Valuable

The other day I had the pleasure of stepping off the face of the earth. A short respite, only hours away from reality, yet its sweetness lingers in my mind.

After a nearby business meeting concluded, my two friends and I needed nourishment, both food and relaxation. We weren't far from a charming Restaurant Inn. Quite unique in a city where everything past any age is routinely torn down to be used as a parking lot. Somehow this building managed to survive contemporary reconstruction. Built so long ago, when the adjacent flour mills depended on the Mississippi River for power to grind the grain and to transport it downstream to the Southern states.

As we entered, the floors creaked beneath us with the footsteps of the thousands preceding ours. The stone hearth, which matched the facade, was assuredly created by workmen eager to settle their families in this new and thriving community.

We caught the dining room between lunch and dinner. How fortunate we were then to be shuttled into the lounge, a cozy room right off the bar. There, sinking into overstuffed chairs, we looked with admiration at the hand painted murals of gentlemen and their ladies sipping glasses of unknown libations. Walls in muted tones highlighted the deep cherrywood panels. The carpeting, visually a work of art in itself, boasted of field flowers landing happily wherever they wished.

We were content, my friends and I, to be immersed in this beauty. Released from the stress of the day, knowing whatever was said—revealed—would be honored with understanding.

We drank a little, ate scrumptious sweet potato fries, and laughed whenever possible.

The sky darkened as rain began to fall. We knew it was time to leave and return to our lives outside this oasis.

The glow of a brass lamp guided our path to the doorway as we reluctantly said our good-byes.

Such a small tender interlude and yet, as we three agreed, nothing we had to do that afternoon was more important than our being there together.

Chocolate After Dark

If ever I were marooned on a desert island, my one chosen companion would not be a handsome movie star. Nor would it be an Eagle Scout who had the ability to rub two sticks together, igniting a fire the Coast Guard could see.

My chosen companion would be Chocolate—the gift the gods have, in all their graciousness, beamed down upon us mortals.

Scooped or slathered or smothered with sauce, chocolate is nearly everyone's favorite flavor. Only a paper wrapper away, it's easy to devour, a reservoir of godly goodness.

Chocolate, the nemesis of the bathroom scale, began its career centuries ago in Mexico as humble cacao pods. During the Aztec Civilization, the royal chef (presumably) ground these tiny seeds into a beverage (the forerunner of cocoa) to please his king, Montezuma, who in turn had forty wives to please. As the story goes, he convinced himself that consuming large quantities of this "potion" gave him the endurance needed to "accommodate" his entire entourage (hence a forerunner of the little blue pill).

Spanish explorers, aware of its quality, brought the bean back to Europe where the elite enjoyed it. Eventually a clever fellow from Switzerland named Nestlé thought to add sugar, and chocolate became everybody's everything. The popularity and prosperity of this new-found sweet escalated into an everyday enjoyment, no longer merely the indulgence of the rich and famous.

Many entrepreneurs have built fortunes on this single flavor. The most famous, of course, is Milton Hershey who, after his caramel business got sticky, switched to chocolate. He introduced customers to the revolutionary five-cent candy bar and developed a quick-energy snack for the military, among many other products.

There are endless examples of chocolate enterprise. Even I dipped into the challenge. Sometimes brilliance comes when least expected, perhaps on a starry night or when I'm in my robe and slippers stirring a cup of coffee. There it was, my million-dollar idea to get rich quick.

The concept was as simple as it was delicious. I would create the Chocolate Spoon for all to enjoy. My prototype was a plastic spoon filled with melted dark chocolate. Placed on waxed paper until hardened, I would then press a chocolate decoration such as a heart or flower on the surface using a drop of softened chocolate as the "glue."

When the chocolate had set up, I'd slip this little work of art into a cello bag and tie it with a colorful ribbon. On the back I'd put a label instructing the user to dip the spoon into hot coffee or warm milk, wait for the chocolate to melt and then—Wow! Enjoy a mocha-java drink!

The spoon could be used again—that is, until the cheap plastic handle snapped off. All this for a buck!

I set myself up in business, ordering thousands of spoons and bags in anticipation. My kitchen became infiltrated. Everywhere I looked I saw spoons: red ones, blue ones, every color ones. They appeared in my head as I slept. Spoons danced in my dreams like a Disney animation. Some even grew faces and smiled at me as though they knew a secret.

Orders poured in like melted chocolate. My right wrist actually looked more trim, thanks to constant exercise. Or perhaps it was my imagination due to lack of sleep.

However, the novelty began to wear down as I began to wear out. One day I packed up the remaining spoons and donated them to a charity where they could make themselves useful on picnics in the park. I then ate the remaining chocolate as consolation, giving up all hope of being listed in Forbes Wealthiest Five Hundred.

But I never abandoned that brown gold. For many years I taught classes in chocolate. The students would assemble early, each trying to grab a front row seat, hoping to be first when samples were passed around.

The room was chillingly quiet, allowing every word of instruction to be absorbed. Most of all I remember the students' eyes, intently watching as I prepared those coveted brownies. I'd stir quickly, sensing the crowd was becoming anxious. I was only one person. They were many.

Dark velvety pies, counters of sweet cupcakes drenched in milk chocolate icing, and mountains of buttery pastries oozing with chocolaty swirls were displayed before them. Their eyes spoke the language of love as they focused on the approaching platters. I saw countless hands, each clenching a single fork, posed to plunge into decadence.

Complete silence followed except for the clicking of silverware. Perhaps an occasional sigh was heard as mounds of silken smooth truffles tickled oh-so-slowly down the palate, teasing each taste bud, pleading for more. Please, just one mouthful more.

I'd smile, knowing happiness filled the air, along with the groans of those who ate too much. People wiped their chins and brushed their shirts, thereby erasing all public evidence of their guilty pleasure.

Class adjourned. Without trepidation, I'd walk to my car in the darkened parking lot, confident the crowd was satisfied. There would be no sarcastic note left on my windshield or chalk marks on the tires. My reputation was solid as a chocolate bar. I had delivered.

Chocolate has even made it to Hollywood, appearing in a 1940's film. *The Chocolate Soldier* is an operetta about a war between Eastern European countries (which doesn't sound like anything to sing about). Obviously the chocolate soldier himself was portrayed by an actual human actor because otherwise he would have melted under the hot lights.

Sorry I cannot interpret the complete libretto for you; I don't speak Bulgarian. I assume, however, that the composer who created all this was inspired by his sweet tooth.

In clothing too, the mere mention of the word *chocolate* denotes high fashion. Change plain "brown" into luxurious chocolaty tones, and that leather jacket goes up a numeral in price.

I must admit there is a downside. Chocolate, as in fudge, is a "nosher's" utopia. But in another context the word "fudge" implies fibbing, as in "who ate the last piece of candy?" We won't pursue this questioning any further.

Each spring I look forward to biting the ears off a chocolate rabbit. This seems to be a popular, though seasonal, activity that many enjoy. I have observed experienced chompers dislodge the bunny's ears swiftly with front teeth extended in an initial attempt. Novices nibble self-consciously while tim-idly working downward. No matter the method, the head of the hare is soon bare.

This concludes my dissertation on chocolate because that bag of chips in the pantry is calling my name. I bought it to make cookies for the children but...

Perhaps you, too, have chocolate hiding in your home. Here's to happy hunting.

I wish your life be filled with sweetness and to all my chocoholic friends, I send you a basket of candy kisses.

May we meet someday in Hershey, PA.

Hot 'n Gooey Fudge Dessert

⅓ cup vegetable oil
4 extra large eggs
1 cup sugar
1 cup cake flour
½ cup cocoa
2 teaspoons baking powder
¼ teaspoon baking soda
½ cup milk
1 teaspoon vanilla

Beat oil, eggs and sugar until mixture is light.

Sift flour with cocoa, baking powder and soda. Add to egg mixture alternately with milk and vanilla. Beat until just blended.

Bake 350° for 40 minutes in a greased bundt pan. Cool for 15 minutes and then invert onto rack. Serve swimming blissfully in Fudge Sauce.

Fudge Sauce

4 1-ounce squares unsweetened baking chocolate
2 tablespoons butter
½ cup strong black coffee
¾ cup sugar
¼ cup corn syrup
1 tablespoon Kaluha

Melt chocolate with butter and blend well. Pour in coffee. Blend sugar with corn syrup in separate bowl.

Combine all ingredients and transfer to a small nonstick saucepan. Boil, uncovered, for 5 minutes, stirring often.

Remove from heat, stir thru Kaluha. Let stand a few hours to thicken.

EVERYTHING'S COMIN' UP ROSIE

The room was dark, almost opaque, in contrast to the startling brightness of a noonday in July. I entered cautiously, concerned that I, too, would be swallowed up by the gloom. But I couldn't retreat and risk being left alone. The others didn't seem to mind, didn't seem to even notice, as though they had always existed in a space without light.

I held tight to the hand of my grandmother—my reason for being there—as she introduced me to her companions of the afternoon, although it did no good because they all looked the same to me. Ancient. Women in similar cotton dresses imprinted with flowers never seen in any garden. Their voluminous skirts, draped over nyloned legs, nearly reached the top of their "Red Cross" shoes. That's what the style was called, apparently in tribute to the humanitarian organization. The footwear was sensible and sturdy, and most women owned at least two pairs, for they acknowledged the seasons as well. The black ones were to be worn during colder months, and the white pair from June through August. These shoes served as a walking calendar, visual from yards away.

Though this assortment of "girls," as they referred to themselves, resembled one another, their voices were in separate octaves, ranging from a husky secret smoker to a shrill soprano who, when excited, sounded like she was sitting on her knitting needles.

The Grande Dame of this "club" was our hostess, Rosie Rosen, owner of the house along with Mosie Rosen (who had chosen to avoid the afternoon's festivity).

Rosie, my grandmother's friend, was a plump, sweet-faced woman with hair so tight to her head that her curlers left obvious indentions.

Crossing the room quickly, her white shoes squeaking, Rosie asked everyone to sit. Except me. As there were more people than furniture, I was demoted to the ottoman, a clumsy, maroon-colored velvet footstool that matched its equally cumbersome chair.

Conversation droned on, and I learned why the room was kept dark. Everyone agreed that keeping the heavy drapes closed and suffering in darkness was preferable to enduring the summer heat. They never imagined that an air-conditioned future was just beyond them.

More important was their topic of conversation: who knew what about whom. Grandma would occasionally put a finger to her lips indicating that I was present. But it didn't matter because I wasn't listening.

I was far more intrigued with my new pastime, that of poking at the braiding along the edges of my seat to see how much dust would rise. My fingers continued to prod deeper into the material until the gray vapors began to fly freely and I feared being discovered.

About that time I heard Rosie say the magic words: Ice Cream. A special treat because no one had a home freezer then, and unless a person lived near a drugstore, such frozen delights were hard to come by.

Luckily, Rosie Rosen did live right across the alley and

around the next corner from such an establishment. Apparently she had pre-arranged this delicious surprise because within minutes a young fellow in a white pharmacy jacket came rushing into the kitchen. With an outstretched arm he held a tin-handled white carton oozing from the bottom. The coveted ice cream was escaping from every fold of the cardboard container despite the runner's flushed face and gasping breath.

Rosie had anticipated the urgency, and small bowls and spoons were set out for each guest. She had been assured that "Neapolitan" was the only choice available, which conveniently allowed the local dairy to avoid criticism from those patrons who were partial to chocolate or vanilla.

Grandma made sure I got all three flavors, and we ate fast before our bowls filled with "soup."

The women chatted as I slipped away to investigate the other areas: bedrooms, neat and tidy and similar in size. In the closest room, propped on the bed, was a large shiny pillow decorated with what the artist hoped was a rose, announced ownership. A corner vanity table covered with jars and pink powder puffs were tempting to touch, but I thought it best to continue snooping out the next room. It had a plain white spread on a plain brown bed which matched the heavy mahogany dresser. Piled high on a nightstand were books with medical titles I couldn't understand but, I imagined, would put anyone to sleep.

I walked back into the hallway. That's when I first saw the photograph of Mosie. He glared out at me as if he were questioning why I was staring back at him. I was transfixed by his black button eyes peering over a long nose. His nostrils were as pinched as his smile. He was hanging there, authoritatively, in a narrow frame with the words "Mosie Rosen, DDS" inscribed along the bottom. So Mosie was a dentist. No wonder his grimace was perfunctory.

I heard Grandma calling me, and I ran back to the maroon room to see the ladies tugging at their midsections. I assumed they had eaten too much ice cream until someone admitted her girdle was squeezing. Another agreed it must be the heat. They all decided it was time to go home.

After dutifully thanking Rosie, Grandma and I walked to the streetcar stop.

"Do Rosie and Mosie have kids?" I asked.

Grandma laughed and replied, "Oh no, dear. They're brother and sister. Mosie owns the house, and Rosie takes care of everything for him. It's been a good arrangement for years."

I was stunned. They shared a home, they shared the same last name, they shared their lives and got along just fine.

Though I never went back to Rosie and Mosie Rosen's house, the impression remained vivid. I marveled how a brother and sister could live together in harmony, so I told my own brother about them and asked how he'd like living always and forever with me.

The look on his face said it all.

For People of a Certain Age –

Who's This Alexa? And What's She Doing In My Home?

If the city was ever to erect a Museum of Natural History for Humans, I surely would be on display.

Exhibited along with Brontosaurus, I am a Dinosaur Obsolete in the land of technology, waiting for another Big Bang to propel me into existence.

I will not apologize for my antiquity. The problem began the day I was born—too soon, decades before the word "internet" was even imagined, let alone became a way of life, and shockingly, even before the word "television" was spoken by the common man.

At the time my generation entered this world—and several generations before us—conversations were connected by operators controlling telephones, usually a woman who obligingly connected your request to "please speak to Aunt Millie in Milwaukee." The operator also retained the authority to listen to the conversation and interrupt with the request to "add more money to continue speaking."

Way back then, the local newspaper was the ultimate source of information, its only competition being the back yard fence where vital, jaw-dropping news was interspersed among windblown sheets and dad's boxer shorts.

Which updates us to the radio, a wooden box decorated with a cloth covering the speaker. Available in a choice of sizes ranging from table top to an imposing cabinet, which was often placed conspicuously in the living room. That made sense, for the device dominated the family's activities. Although the radio did transmit occasional "fireside chats", its main purpose was entertainment. An astute eye could detect crumbs deposited by the after-school snackers; however, such spillage was frequently the residue of late-night sandwiches consumed by elders while listening to the swing bands and imagining that they, too, were in New York's Savoy Ballroom.

Although it now seems inadequate, we who participated in that era got along fine. Or at least we thought so, until television bombarded our contentment and thrust us into a sea of communications.

More intrusive than a radio, TV came to town amidst gasps and giggles. We no longer had to imagine how the ingénue valiantly fought the advances of a handsome rogue who meant her no good. It was there, right before our eyes. Of course her purity was spared—right after the final commercial.

We sat spellbound, in awe, as we glared at the television set across the room. We questioned how all these pictures, all this visual stuff, could be transmitted through clumsy cables. Before long we were astounded to discover that color, too, was possible, for the initial programming had been entirely black and white. What genius coaxed the rainbow into this picturama?

Holy Handset. The ultimate pleasure of a remote control became a bedside companion. No longer did we need to extricate ourselves from the comfort of a warm blanket to run across the room to change the channel. Our only alternative was to leave the set on all night and waken to the 6 a.m. meteorologist.

Life was excellent. We had a printed agenda of what to watch when, and our forefinger poised on the channel of choice. Add a cold beer and call it heaven.

Yet great minds couldn't leave it there. The initial ripples of even higher technology began streaking across the dawn, awakening naïve minds to a complexity of choice. What was to follow would have amazed mid-twentieth intellects as something out of science fiction. Most people would no sooner have envisioned grabbing a phone from their pocket than pulling a rabbit out from their hat. This magical phone, capable of filming an event, could also take pictures that introduced the word "selfie" to our vocabulary. Words such as "tweet" and "e-mail" and iPhone began to appear regularly in conversation. As an ancient fossil, I thought they referenced birds communicating with one another while the "e" before mail meant efficient delivery. Certainly there should be no debate that the once popular blackberry, associated with jam, partners well with toast. And that's all we'll say about that.

A small, square object recently arrived at my house, a birthday gift from my family to entertain me. Introduced to me as Alexa, I shout orders and she does what I request. Alexa behaves better than my children ever did.

The largest life-altering explosion was, of course, the Internet. It influenced our economy; it enlarged our view of the world and the entire way in which we live our lives. Even the word "mouse" took on new meaning. No longer referring to a small gray creature capable of provoking adults to screech in protest, this "mouse" guides us on our quest for knowledge. How so many facts can be masked behind a screen is beyond my comprehension. Perhaps the same wizard who turns on the refrigerator light also hides in my computer with a stash of information.

Yes, I'm just joking to disguise my inability to understand the concept. My own computer defies me, often reverting to a screen of flowers. It's so much harder than changing the ribbon on my typewriter. I continue to press the keyboard until, out of options, I call my grandson who advises me to "re-boot," which means to give it a rest, then try gain. I relax, unplug the thing and pay him in chocolate chip cookies.

I cling to the memory of yesteryear, when at my convenience I spoke on a "land line" phone and was spared interruptive calls at the dentist's office.

"Zoom" calls are very convenient for those remaining in pajama bottoms with only their top half displayed. This works out well for business meetings, but for many who are aging, appearing without make-up in stark lighting is undeniably lousy. Better to hear only the lilt of another's voice and picture them in eternal youth.

With this nostalgia I fondly remember receiving handwritten notes, a gesture of thoughtfulness for something I did that made someone feel better. It makes me feel better too, and I often leave the cards nearby to be re-read on a dreary day.

Younger generations will be privileged to witness wonders yet to be discovered, phenomenas to be explored still unknown to our ingenuity.

That is their gift of tomorrow. Today our lives are saturated with lightning enlightenment. But for "people of a certain age," pushing our comfortable margins—the limits that have worked for us this far—are unsettling. We attempt to absorb, to comprehend the bewildering, and we assure both ourselves and those observing us that, we too are smart enough, capable enough to re-boot ourselves.

It's hard work. Among a myriad of possibilities we must learn a new language and new techniques. It's a challenge to remember which button to push and what not to touch.

Sometimes we feel foolish, inadequate, as we observe a toddler at a nearby table obsessed with his plastic computer.

"What chance do we have?" we joke to one another.

We leave it at that, a laugh at ourselves, then go home—and try again.

My Pal Sal

"I wonder what became of Sally?" Is this merely the title of a classic Jerome Kern musical, or is it a nostalgic longing for a lost friend?

I'll tell you the story. Then you can judge for yourself.

Many years ago, when I was still young enough to believe what I read, I nonchalantly paged through a magazine.

Now, you ask, why was this newsworthy? Well, towards the back of this publication was an advertisement that made such an impression, my life was never quite the same again.

A long skinny column read: "Banana Plants for Sale." It continued: "You can be the proud owner of a horticultural wonder! For only [and I've conveniently forgotten the price] you'll enjoy your very own banana bush! Within weeks, you'll be feasting on this tasty fruit known to be rich in potassium and easily digestible, too." The hard-sell continued with a picture of smiling parents and smiling children gathered together in front of a television set, munching contentedly on what appeared to be bananas. The caption underneath sealed the deal: "Now you, too, can eat bananas while watching TV!"

I was intrigued. Nobody in my social circle had ever tried growing a tropical fruit in a northern kitchen. I would be a trendsetter. At my next neighborhood soiree, I would mingle among the other guests, extolling my new adventure.

With anticipation, I filled out the order form, enclosed the appropriate check, and mailed off the envelope. As promised, within four to six weeks an unobtrusive package arrived. Quickly, I tore off the brown wrapping paper, ripped open the cardboard box, and uncovered a very small greenery potted in a cheap plastic cup. "Welcome home, my little banana bonanza!" It was the first of many affectionate sentences I would say to that plant. I had always heard that vegetation needs the same kind words of encouragement we humans do.

I placed my new houseguest in the sunny bay window of the kitchen and conscientiously watered it every other day. After a while (and this was not my imagination), the plant actually developed a personality. As it grew under my meticulous nurturing, it required an individual identity, a name of its own.

Without hesitation, I called her "Sally." I don't know why. She just looked like a "Sally" to me.

Weeks evolved into months, and Sally kept getting larger. It became necessary to re-pot her from small to big to "Hey, she's overtaken the entire bay window!" Her branches protruded at incongruous angles, giving her an endearing absurdity. Surely, her ancestors had been jungle inhabitants. The day came when I was forced to tie her lower branches together so no one would trip as they walked by.

Yes, Sally was big and bushy and beautiful—but unfortunately not bountiful. Never once did I see a single banana bloom. Even as her massive leaves began to flop over onto the kitchen table, there was no indication of success. Sally just sat there, steadfast in the sunlight, guzzling water, but never offering anything in return.

I began to question if it was my fault. Maybe I hadn't watched enough television to give her an incentive. Maybe I should have tried tough love instead of cooing sweet praise each day.

Or maybe Sally was a hoax, merely a misrepresentation

by greedy pitchmen eager to raise expectations and grab money from gullible customers.

Maybe they knew all along that if I craved a banana, I'd still have to go to a grocery store.

Well, I continued to coax her to reproduce, but as you know, life moves at a rapid pace. Summer approached and I was scheduled to attend cooking school in Paris. Even Sally couldn't hold me back from such a commitment. My teenage son volunteered to stay home and run the household, which included watering the plants. Off I went, and there he stayed—fully focused on having great fun while Mom was away. I needn't go into detail because many of us have experienced similar situations.

When I returned home later that summer, Sally was no longer with us. I came in the door, threw down my carry-on, rushed into the kitchen, and called out her name. But my once-luxurious foliage was merely a dried-up skeleton of her former self.

A brittle, brown leaf shattered at my touch. I ran for water, crying out, "Sally, Sally, I'm home now, you're safe!" But it was too late. Survival was no longer an option.

Poor Sally died of thirst that summer during the same months my son and his friends frolicked on the beach. I must admit, when I returned home, I was relieved to see the house was still standing.

After resting from the trip, I said a gentle goodbye to my pal, Sal. I carted her remains to the back of the yard and carefully extracted her from the pot she'd dwelled in. With a fond adieu, I placed Sally in the alley. Her eulogy was short; I forgave her for letting me down—for even at the end, there was not a hint of fruit revealed in the depths of her shrubbery. I loved her just the same. And, if it were possible, I sensed she'd have felt a fondness for me, too.

Her enormous pot was donated to charity—hopefully to assist someone else with a greener thumb than mine.

Over the years, Sally has faded into a sweet memory. On occasion, my mind wanders back to her when I'm standing in the produce section of a food market and see a counter generously laden with bananas of all descriptions—some still green, others already speckled with ripeness.

I think of Sally, too, on quiet nights when I settle in to watch television and wish for a snack. It is then that I walk into the kitchen and reluctantly make myself microwave popcorn.

With a twinge of sadness, I remember what could have been....

REALLY GOOD BANANA BREAD

2 ½ cups sugar
1 cup butter
4 extra large eggs
2 cups bananas, mashed
3 cups flour
1 cup buttermilk
2 teaspoons baking soda
½ teaspoon salt
2 teaspoons vanilla
Chopped walnuts

Cream sugar and butter. Add eggs and bananas. Blend in flour, alternating with buttermilk, which has been combined with soda.

Add salt and vanilla. Blend well. Fold in walnuts.

Grease two 9 x 5" loaf pans. Pour batter into pans. Bake at 350° about 35-40 minutes.

Note: Adding mini-chocolate chips would be a nice variation. Also makes really great muffins and freezes well.

Snake Lake

"Joe and his big ideas!" Their voices bellowed in unison, for no one in the family could figure out where these ideas came from or how it could be happening to them.

Joe, the father of them all, was building a lake house for his relatives who didn't swim or surf or know how to steer a boat.

Here was a family whose happiness was sitting in a robe and reading, perhaps with a little background music and a small libation on the chair arm. Involved in the art scene, constantly immersed in creative projects, they were content to paint the sky and water blending into the sunset. The very thought of wandering into the picture themselves never occurred to them.

But their affection for Joe exceeded their reluctance to participate, so they permitted this obtuse intrusion into their habitually indoor lifestyle.

Patriarch Joe had secretly longed to own a place near the water, a gathering for family and friends. He felt the time was now or never. So at his seventieth birthday celebration when everyone was present he astounded them all by unrolling the blueprints. The "ooohs and ahhhs" brought a smile to Joe's face. He had designed a large living/kitchen area and bedrooms on both the main level and below. With the addition of sleeping bags, there'd be enough room to accommodate everybody. Joe explained that the speedboat would be tied to a lengthy deck, while a nearby shack was going to be filled with inflatable toys and water skis.

He had thought of everything. Everything, that is, except the reaction of his family (those devotees of comfort and convenience) to life in the North Woods.

"Dad, whoever said we wanted a lake house? You know we're not the outdoor type. Our 'outdoors' is having lunch on the patio."

Another voice reaffirmed with, "We walk from the house to the car!"

Conversation would have continued, but their father's expression stopped everyone in mid-sentence. Not wanting to be unappreciative, they quickly reverted to a positive tone.

"Thanks, Dad, what a great place to share! All of us together, every weekend the whole summer long!"

Others in the room feigned a smile.

The contractor kept on schedule so that by spring of the following year, the house was ready. It was located on a northern lake that a long-forgotten official had named "Snake" although no reptiles had ever been found. Said official undoubtedly thought himself brilliant to chose a name that rhymed with "Lake."

Joe was exhilarated, while shopping for pine furniture, to spot an ensemble with naugahyde upholstery imprinted with moose silhouettes and assorted fish (of no known species) leaping out from nowhere.

A massive stone fireplace along one wall was filled with logs for evenings when a chill filled the air. The cupboards were stacked with plastic dishes and casseroles large enough for twenty portions.

Down on the waterfront the speedboat, securely tied, bobbed patiently as it waited to begin its maiden voyage until somebody figured out the instruction manual.

Joe and his wife, Sarah, made the plan. They would drive to Snake Lake on Thursdays from Memorial Day until early September. Arriving before the others would give them time to prepare. Fresh produce, sold along the roadside, would be purchased, along with the giant cinnamon rolls from the hole-in-the wall bakery nearby. The others could bring up the steaks for the grill along with their loyal companions, Samuel Adams and Jack Daniels.

Joe and Sarah got a late start that first Thursday. They did stop to pick up tomatoes and potatoes at the farmer's road stand but lost their cinnamon rolls to earlier customers. The bakery was down to rhubarb pie, which nobody liked, so they settled on a selection of muffins and hurried on their way.

Arriving after dark with just enough energy to throw sheets on the beds, they fell asleep so soundly they didn't hear the warning signals blare. Ominous weather was approaching. A call from their son alerted them that a tornado was heading their way.

As quickly as seniors can run, they settled into the lower level. Joe waited for further calls from the caravan of family cars already en route. A few were safely inside city limits and could turn back. But the lead group had traveled too far on the highway.

After some minutes (which seemed like hours), another call came from the car in peril. Everyone was shaken but alright. They had pulled under a bridge for safety and, as soon as possible, would head back home.

Joe suggested they continue to the lake but realized he had a losing argument.

"Enough already, Dad! Everybody's still frightened. We'll try again, sometime. Stay safe."

With that, the call ended. For the next three days Joe and Sarah spent a quiet weekend consuming a quantity of tomatoes and muffins.

With such a dramatic initiation, Joe had difficulty convincing the family the weather had merely played a quirky trick. This time, it was decided, they would travel together in family SUVs. And on the following Friday afternoon three vehicles drove dutifully northward, arriving at the house Joe had built in time for dinner. A delectable array of steaks and burgers were ready for the grill. The only problem was that the grill wasn't ready to perform. Everyone had assumed someone else was bringing the briquettes. Instead they put together a nice meal of calico salad, relishes, and buns.

By ten o'clock everybody had settled down, if only from the evening's mayhem. The children fought over possession of the top bunk-beds, and extra sleeping bags covered all vacant flooring, making it imperative to walk carefully to avoid stepping on a relative.

Next morning the sun shone brightly, inviting the way to outdoors and challenging everyone to participate in the day's activities. All, that is, except Sarah, who insisted she'd stay indoors to make cheese blintzes for the crowd. It had long been her signature dish, but no one thought it would become her constant activity. Sarah persisted, wishing everyone a good time while she remained at her solitary post, alone in the quiet, and she continued this behavior all summer, insisting this was her contribution. Occasionally she ventured out to the porch for a short visit.

Several of the men attempted to conquer the speed-boat. They took turns reading the owner's guide, each reciting key points to the other. With minimal confidence they started the ignition. Two teen cousins stood ready on skis for a glide across the waters. It began well. The boat lunged forward with enough velocity, and the boys were up and away. How impressive they looked for more than a minute before losing their grip and splashing downward. As they swam to safety, the erratic speedboat spontaneously zig-zagged around before struggling towards shore. Somehow one of the "sailors" aboard docked the wayward vessel.

All who witnessed them cheered for the courageous sea-men. At lunch that day, it was unanimously decided to purchase a slow and steady pontoon. Those who chose could then fish. That arrangement didn't work out for long, however, because only one aunt agreed to clean and scrape the scales, and she had resigned by July. Therefore fish frys were limited to whatever the nearby convenience store featured that week.

The "week-end" multiplied into "week-ends." As the summer progressed, so did everyone's prowess. The speedboat no longer outsmarted them, and the water skiers maintained their balance. In time even the dogs settled down. The little ones stopped yelping, and the larger ones stopped sniffing them. All who came often brought friends, and there always seemed to be enough space and blintzes for everyone. Most got along much of the time. They were too far from home to conjure up an unexpected alibi for an early exit.

Of course, there was the time Joe needed immediate help

with a loose screen. His teenage grandson preferred to linger over lunch and, after a brusque exchange, the boy stormed out, determined to walk back to the city. He was retrieved before he'd reached the mailbox. Lesson learned.

That same screen remained insignificant until a five-year-old had nothing better to do than lean against it. Suddenly the screen tore away from the window frame, hurling the child out onto the grassy slope below. Joe set a record dashing out to grab him. The child recovered from his minor bruises and convalesced en route to the Dairy Queen.

Swimming was a challenge. Gobs of greenish algae thick-ened the water, discouraging the "toe dippers" as it attached to their ankles and turned their feet green.

The languorous warmth of summer evolved into the golden crispness of autumn. It was time to close the lake house for the winter. Joe and Sarah made the final trip north. Lawn chairs were stored, along with the "hammock for two," a favorite hide-out for the lazy. One of them had devised the clever technique of tying a rope around the nearest tree so that the lounger could pull on it for perpetual rocking. Shaded by foliage, this comfortable nest provided quiet moments to read or hug a child or just watch the clouds drift by.

Yes, it was time to lock the door and look forward to the following spring. But before he left, Joe shivering in his plaid bathing suit, took one final bath in the chilled lake waters.

On the drive home, he and Sarah spoke honestly. They knew they had been pushing it all summer. Whether it was DNA or environmental tendencies, this collection of relatives did not carry the "fit in frolic" gene. Their idea of activity was playing miniature golf. But they would do anything to please

Joe. He sat comfortably in his driver's seat, feeling the love.

The lake house weekends continued for many years, though everyone scattered down separate paths eventually. It was okay to let go. Dream fulfilled. Joe had been so proud of his hospitality home, overcrowded with a boisterous entourage.

On somebody's bookshelf there's an album of photos occasionally opened to the same comments and laughter.

"How young—and thin—we all were!" Then the pages are closed until the next time someone remembers to bring it out.

So it remains. Pages of sweet nostalgia of the hapless, yet well meaning.

Let's hear it for the outdoor enthusiasts and a bug spray salute to those nimble sports as they have their UV30 day in the sun.

Me? I'll cheer for that guy on the couch.

May air conditioning reign forever.

Tea and Me

The hallway was long, with unexpected twists and turns. I walked rapidly alongside my friend, eager to reach our final destination. Loud footsteps indicated our approach; the thunder of clumsy Oxford shoes colliding with cement flooring. Ladies shouldn't clomp along that loudly, but we were not yet ladies and really didn't care about fracturing social etiquette.

My friend of the day (anyone in class who would accompany me) and I continued along the lengthy corridor until we finally reached the door of the restaurant. Amazed at our accomplishment, we stood for a moment admiring the replicas of gray plastic rocks placed strategically around the entrance. Apparently a decorator with questionable taste had installed them. They looked cumbersome, but their appearance created the intended impression that we were entering a cave. Mysterious and intriguing—though to some it might have appeared peculiar—the entrance was, to two teenage girls, straight out of a movie.

With a sprinkle of exaggeration added, our lunch surely would become the talk of the girls' locker room on Monday. Evoking jealousy, if possible.

We stood silently, pretending to admire an especially odd-shaped boulder to our left, when we were approached by an equally odd-looking woman, presumably the hostess. Dressed as the Gypsy Queen, or her rendition of one, the woman's long black gown was offset with panels of gold-threaded embroidery. A set of large glittering earrings matched the necklace dangling capriciously over her ample bosom. Her face was plastered with make-up in a futile attempt to disguise her age. The rouge on her cheeks only accented their sagginess; nothing could hide the years. But her smile as she greeted us was friendly. We were welcomed guests as she escorted us to a corner table away from the clanging in the kitchen. The windowless room was equally gray, lit only by small vintage lamps on each table, presumably to enhance the adventure.

"Sit here, girls. Enjoy your lunch. Would you like a reading afterwards?"

I nodded we would. And under my breath whispered to my friend that was the only reason we had come here.

It surely wasn't for the food. A culinary school dropout was undoubtedly head chef. With probable ingredients from government surplus, the menu was far left of gourmet. But we trusted the city's health inspector to keep us safe so we proceeded to order.

"We'll both have the chow mein, please. And, of course, tea. We need those tea leaves for our reading."

We sat back and waited for our food, if it could be categorized as such. "Chow Mein" was simply a conglomeration—vegetables of unknown origin assembled over packaged noodles. It was the restaurant's star entrée. Which indicates the level of their haute cuisine.

We ate as much as we could, sipped our teas, and then signaled the Gypsy Queen that we were "ready."

She nodded so vigorously her golden earrings shook in compliance.

Within minutes a Gypsy fortune teller approached our table. At least that's the impression she was going for. Similar to the hostess, she was dressed in a long skirt. Her shoulders were draped in a flowered scarf with multi-colored tassels cascading down. Tied around her head was another smaller scarf that did not match anything at all. But it served the purpose of hiding the gray roots of her black hair. Her face was kindly, as though she already knew why we had come to endure lunch. She would not disappoint.

"Hello, I'm Estrelitta," a name I didn't believe. (I doubt she did either.) After checking our tea cups to see if we had consumed enough, Estrelitta proceeded to read our futures from the soggy leaves. My friend was first to hear how she would excel in school and have a fine career as a certified public accountant. This sounded strange to me as I knew her to barely pass algebra, but I was too excited to hear my own prediction to interfere.

My turn at last. There was no talk of academics. Instead, Estrelitta zoomed in on what I wanted to hear: I would meet a stranger; no, he would not necessarily be tall and dark, but definitely new to me. Of course we'd be smitten with one another and, avoiding all of life's usual pitfalls, live together on the sunny side of the street.

Deliberately oblivious to the reality that damp leaves on the bottom of a cup could foretell the future, we were content with Estrelitta's insight and wanted to believe she was true blue.

Having fulfilled her obligation to us, she then rose, pausing just long enough for a gratuity before disappearing somewhere in the room, presumably to fill another's fantasy about meeting my stranger's brother and living next door to us in Pleasantville.

My friend, the supposed math expert, and I grinned with satisfaction. We left the restaurant, stopped for an ice cream (as we were still hungry) and then took the bus home.

Many years have since passed. These visits to a Gypsy Cave linger only in my mind on a quiet evening before sleep. A dashing stranger did not bedazzle me with a life of luxury, nor did my friend ever enter the world of higher finance. The restaurant has long since disappeared, vanishing without a trace. It simply "poofed" itself into non-existence, abandoning that wandering corridor to nowhere.

Could the site have been transformed into a hide-out for the unscrupulous? Or did the landlord use it for storage? The local news never covered the story.

Somewhere in a city dump the fragments of those pseudo-rocks may still exist. Reduced to ashes, their gray dust could still be infiltrating the air we inhale today.

Those women, that charade of characters who tried desperately to be fascinating, have dissolved into memories. Their colorful Gypsy scarves are now relics in an antique store.

But credit must be given. More show biz than real, they offered their patrons a passage to the unknown. If only to tip-toe into the future and flirt with what might be.

It was a lot to digest, back then. Along with that lousy chow main.

The Beauty of Being Alone

I awaken to silence. The same quiet to which I closed my eyes last night.

The morning ritual begins. I am on automatic pilot: the toothbrush, the hairbrush, a quick shower, and a cup of something to get me going.

I swallow the silkiness of my herbal tea, allowing the warm liquid to slide slowly downward, lubricating my voice. Who would I speak to today? Will I give words of wisdom, comfort to a friend experiencing life's raw edges, or will I speak tough love to a young person who needs to do some serious growing up?

Sunbeams do their best to brighten the room, combating the obstinate Midwest pallor. Outside, a wind blows through a tree; its barren branches defy movement, holding strong against the challenge of repeated battering.

I am that tree. I know that I draw my resiliency from a gift I often give myself. Time alone. Time reserved to stop, catch my breath and get a fresh perspective. Our lives are on overload, and this "escapism" isn't easy. But for me, being alone—by myself, for myself—is rejuvenating. I cannot become fragmented by the criteria of others.

The clock ticks, but I am not yet hungry. I will eat when I please and leave the empty plate on the kitchen counter if I wish.

The music blares, but no one hollers, "Turn that damn noise off!" It is my brass section, and I like it loud.

My clothes fit loosely, and my socks don't match. It gives me joy.

Stretching to be charming and "on point" is demanding. Life is like a circus, and no one can maintain the center ring for long. We do the best we can—in business, with family, and in our community. We give until there's a hollow inside. To balance this vacuum, we need to steal time to recuperate.

I call this "healthy selfishness": preserving corners of my live, re-igniting my spirit with untapped possibilities.

It's refreshing to relax and allow my mind to wander into hidden places, with thoughts not to be shared because they belong to nobody else.

I am the caretaker of my secret memories, images of people and happenings too important to forget.

My home is peaceful today. The aura of calm surrounds me. I am content with the company of one, for I am the proud owner of me.

Tomorrow I will rejoin the marathon. Maybe.

The popcorn is buttered. The sofa awaits me.

THE COLLECTION DETECTION

The architect of my home must have been Edgar Allan Poe. I say this because the walls seem to be closing in on me, slowly yet deliberately. This imprisonment threatens me as I recollect Poe's classic tale in which his character was in jeopardy of being crunched to a sorrowful conclusion.

One day it may happen to me, along with countless others plagued by the same tendency: We can't give anything away. Our reasoning is that we might need it someday.

There's a large group of us known as "savers" who need to be saved, released from holding on to a precious possession such as a salad bowl shaped like a coliseum.

Common sense and an over-crowded shelf have no influence. "Tossing out" is a lost art form meant for those who lead prudent lives. To me, the sight of a closet jam-packed with garments teetering on a sagging pole is poetry in motion.

Yes, there are collectors of fine art, rare stamps, and the pictorial life of Lincoln. I do not, however, fall into that respected category. I simply am a collector of collections.

I cannot blame this habit on a deprived childhood, one in which I owned one tattered, hand-me-down dress, thereby justifying my excuse to overcompensate today.

Nope. There was nothing sad about my youth. I just hold on to "things."

By now many of you must be nodding in empathy.

Years ago, when I traded my family home for a compact condo I was forced to confront a reduction of all worldly goods. Three piles, or shall I say "mountains," were created: one to discard, another for charity, and the final to take along because I could not live without the contents.

It all seemed clear. The intention, the opportunity confronted me. I rose to the occasion and the "stuff" and I parted ways. I took what I needed; I left what I didn't.

"A place for everything and everything in its place" could have been a sign upon the door.

That was then; this is now. Slowly, insidiously, merchandise seems to have infiltrated every crevice once again. Although I sleep soundly, I am suspicious that invisible creatures creep silently during the night carting Amazon surplus into my home. My once tidy kitchen now bursts with enough cookware to supply a restaurant, defying the cupboard doors to stay shut.

Closets have become safe harbors for clothing I now no longer need, such as formalwear worn to the weddings of couples now celebrating their tenth anniversaries. The only advantage is that a thief would give up in frustration searching for hidden money stashed behind seldom-used luggage.

Maybe on some rainy day I'll force myself to sort through this accumulation and make three new piles: one to toss, another for charity, and a third to jump into for fun.

I honestly can't comprehend how all this excess paraphernalia has appeared out of nowhere. Perhaps there is some mystical power—some abracadabra—that makes walls get smaller and actually shrink down before my eyes. A phenomenon without explanation.

Always the optimist, I do feel there is hidden potential here. I think I'm on to a good thing. All I have to do is capture the essence of its magical properties. Then I would somehow extract that quality of making things diminish and (perhaps with the help of a pharmacist) create a salve to sell to a grateful audience as a panacea for expanding waistlines.

I'll make a fortune.

The Unde-Feeted

Although a sock may be a foot's best friend, it certainly has no connection to my dinner and none whatsoever to my vision.

Please explain why the salmon filet on the plate before me is named "Sock-eye."

Allowing the fish to cool in a puddle of tartar sauce, it provokes thought on how one small word can have so many interpretations.

Although undocumented, it's possible Soc-rates was the father of socks. "When the feet are warm, so is the heart" is an ageless philosophy. Though artifacts indicate his crowd ran around in open-toe sandals, he was smart enough to be a fore-runner.

Continuing our investigation, the term "Sock it away" could mean hiding money or jewels in a secret place. While this excludes a bank, it could involve the back of a closet or, at the very least, a forgotten briefcase.

Socks are diverse. The vision of an oversized stocking appliqued with peppermint candy canes glows in our child-hood memories, a joyful recipient of holiday sweets and small gifts as it hung on the fireplace.

Conversely, a sock can be mysterious, the eternal ques-tion that great minds cannot answer. Two stockings go into the wash; only one comes out. How did the missing mate disappear? Is there a "never-land" over the horizon where socks go to hide from their owners? Never to be seen again, one foot must remain in the cold.

That brings us to another dilemma. A sock could hurt somebody. Take my advice; if you don't agree with someone, just walk away. It's not polite to hit people.

Which brings up hollering at the umpire at a White Sox game. Not all of us are from Chicago, but most of us love baseball. Apparently the team got their name from wearing white stockings which, while sliding into third base, couldn't have remained pristine past the seventh inning. Why they didn't alter their title to the "Dirty Gray Socks" is beyond me.

Take note: a sock-et is not a small sock. Anyone can own a socket—even a very large linebacker. All you have to do is call an electrician.

There you have it. My exploration of socks from patterned hosiery to terrycloth crews, whatever you choose each morning to complete your feet.

It also gives me comfort to know that my toes are well covered when, inevitably, I put my foot in my mouth.